W9-BSA-593

ILLINOIS CENTRAL COLLEGE
PE1475.A63 1982
STACKS
Write for results /

A12900 810631

WITHDRAWN

PE 1475 .A63 1982

12072

Andrews, William D.

Write for results /

Illinois Central College
Learning Resources Center

WRITE FOR RESULTS

- ## William D. Andrews
  Philadelphia College of Textiles and Science

- ## Deborah C. Andrews
  Drexel University

I.C.C. LIBRARY

LITTLE, BROWN AND COMPANY — BOSTON – TORONTO

12072

Library of Congress Cataloging in Publication Data

Andrews, William D. (William David), 1945-
  Write for results.

  Bibliography: p. 109
  Includes index.
  1. English language—Rhetoric. 2. English
language—Technical English. 3. English language—
Business English. I. Andrews, Deborah C. II. Title.
PE1475.A63   808'.042   81-23644
ISBN 0-316-04209-9   AACR2

Copyright © 1982 by Little, Brown and Company (Inc.)

All rights reserved. No part of this book may be repro-
duced in any form or by any electronic or mechanical
means including information storage and retrieval systems
without permission in writing from the publisher, except
by a reviewer who may quote brief passages in a review.

ISBN 0-316-042099

9 8 7 6 5 4 3 2 1

ALP

Published simultaneously in Canada
by Little, Brown & Company (Canada) Limited

Printed in the United States of America

· CONTENTS ·

· LIST OF FIGURES ·

· PREFACE ·

Write for Results is not meant as a textbook on writing for the person who needs practice in basic verbal skills. Rather, it is a guide to better written communication for the professional who finds that most of his or her working life is spent not behind a lab bench or computer terminal or drawing board—as all those years of formal education promised— but at a desk, trying to turn facts and ideas into the readable and persuasive letters, reports, brochures, and proposals that form the real work of any professional.

The guide is short and practical. It is designed to be read on a flight from Chicago to Houston or on a Metroliner from New York to Washington. It may also accompany formal instruction in writing in the college or professional school classroom or the in-house workshop.

The advice we offer here derives from our experience in teaching writing over many years to a wide variety of persons in many settings. We want to thank, then, the many undergraduate, graduate, and professional students we have worked with for a decade and a half at Utah State University, The Ohio State University, the Philadelphia College of Textiles and Science, and Drexel University; and the working professionals from many corporations and public agencies who participated in short courses at these universities and at Battelle Memorial Institute, General Electric Switchgear Division, RCA Government Systems Division, and the Ohio Department of Education.

Paul O'Connell encouraged us to put the outcome of those experiences into writing and then found excellent reviewers whose comments on earlier versions of this guide were immensely helpful and appropriately professional: Kirsten

A. Dodge, Lilian O. Feinberg, John J. Fenstermaker, Barbara F. Nodine, Ellen Nold, and Nancy Sommers. We further appreciate conversations—in our offices, over dinner, in hallways at meetings—with colleagues whose thinking about writing informed and energized our own thinking. We want to thank in particular Margaret D. Blickle, Edward P. J. Corbett, John Harris, and J. C. Mathes. We also thank Donna Trieger for speedy and accurate typing.

We are also grateful to the institutions that provided stimulating homes for us as we worked—the Philadelphia College of Textiles and Science and Drexel University; to our son Christopher Andrews, who made our real home stimulating throughout the work; and to our parents, William and Hazel Andrews and Mark and Gertrude Crehan, who started it all.

WRITE
FOR RESULTS

THE PROCESS OF WRITING

WRITING IS A WAY of transferring information. Developing information, evaluating it, and then telling it to others are common functions of all professionals—lawyers, engineers, scientists, accountants, architects, market analysts, managers, and physicians. Professionals like you are information brokers. Brokering information is your principal task as a professional, the core of the business.

Writing is of course not the only way in which information is transferred. Information transfer occurs orally as conversation, presentation, or lecture; and electronically, as charges on a chip, tape, or disk. This guide, however, concentrates on written transfer, which remains the most common, most basic, and most persuasive form of conveying information from one person to another or to a group.

In this guide writing is viewed as a *process*, only the last stage of which entails the selection of words and the composing of strings of sentences and paragraphs. The first and most difficult challenge professionals face in writing is not putting words on paper but preparing information for transfer. The information is often highly complex and embedded in forms—like computer printouts, blueprints, lab notebooks, statistical reports—that require adjustments for presentation in documents suitable for others to read. Producing a document that works means more than assuring conformance to the dictates of grammar and spelling, although these dictates of course count. It means approaching writing as you do any professional project in which you must select, weigh, contemplate, rearrange, rethink, plan, and assemble. Specifically, the process of writing involves assessing the context for the document and defining the communications problem to be solved, planning the tasks and the document that will solve the problem, and then putting words on paper.

Figure 1.1 provides an overview of the process. The figure shows the three steps—context, planning, and product—as they parallel the route to solving a professional, technical, or scientific problem. You end the first stage with a control statement, a one-sentence summary of the document's message and of the work it will do for the reader. In the second stage, you plan. Really, you need two plans: a management plan of tasks for assembling the document and a writing plan that shows the design of the document itself. The management plan helps get the document done on time and with a minimum of confusion and ill will, especially if several people contribute sections. The document plan schedules material to appear in the document where the reader needs it and where you the writer will gain greatest advantage from it. The plan also distributes material to the appropriate channel of communication—verbal, visual, or mathematical. Writing is linear. Only one item can be presented at a time. In designing the right plan, you test several options for presentation. You move different items in and out of the beginning, middle, and end positions until you achieve a suitable arrangement.

Third, based on a well-structured plan, you write. You put words on paper in a language and style that match the reader's understanding and in an order that accommodates his or her need to act. Once you've completed a draft, you move backward to check the document you have written against the criteria you established.

Of course, much good thinking occurs in the round, not in the simple forward motion shown in figure 1.1. You can

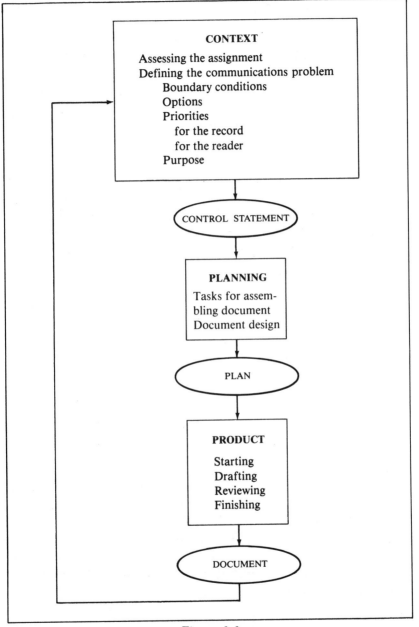

Figure 1.1
The writing process

move back and forth between steps. You can omit a step. For certain documents, you can trace an entirely different pattern. Writing encompasses more than mere skills. It taps one's intuition and emotions. The process is subject at times to whim, inspiration, bouts with the telephone, and indigestion. But the routine presented in this guide provides a baseline for all writing tasks. It allows you to approach writing not as an unmanageable whole but in discrete, functional steps. It also sorts somewhat the wrestling with ideas and information from the wrestling with words in a draft. It should reduce the role of whimsy and put the act of writing on the same level as the process of problem-solving used in your other professional activities.

Communications Model

Each step in the process is the focus of a chapter. Within each chapter, the simple communications model shown in figure 1.2 underlies the discussion. The test of effectiveness and efficiency in a document is its appropriateness to the writer, the material, the reader, and the purpose. As a writer, you will have to assess relative priorities among these forces for each document you write. Sometimes you will have to eliminate information you might like to present because the reader won't understand it. Or you may decide to emphasize the material and address only those readers who can understand. Or you may feel that the uninitiated reader must be addressed, and so you spend the time to adjust material to make it understandable. Throughout the writing, keep these forces in mind:

1. *Writer:* Sometimes you write for yourself, in a journal or log, as a way of seeing how a line of reasoning comes out. The material is shaped to your own needs; the language may be your own private code.

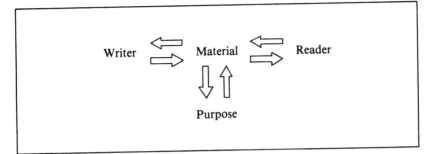

Figure 1.2
Communications model

2. *Material:* Many sections of reports, and some whole documents, are material-based. That is, the writing aims towards invisibility. The information dictates the emphasis and the form. Often material is presented in visuals and numbers rather than words.

3. *Reader:* But for most documents most of the time, when information must be *transferred*, the reader's needs shape the structure for transfer.

4. *Purpose:* Finally, the balance among writer, material, and reader is a function of your purpose:

• *To see what you're thinking?* Let the sentences go where they will; record ideas as they come to you.
• *To record information for reference?* Be complete; shape material in figures and tables; interpret for the record.
• *To win a contract? Convince a client? Foster understanding?* Adjust the structure and language of your material to suit the reader; avoid private codes; select emphasis in your material to match the reader's priorities and ability to assimilate information.

Writing for Readers

In writing to transfer information to readers the aim of most of your writing as a professional is to persuade. The document must be instrumental, directed to get something done, to cause someone to act. Two axioms operate in writing for readers:

If you can be misunderstood, you will be misunderstood.

One small example: the following sentence appeared in a short brochure written by a prestigious consulting firm and distributed by a large insurance company.

The problems which concern most businessmen are those of communication, activists' lack of misunderstanding of how business operates, the role of profits and profit margins, and what are perceived (among the minority) as the unrealistic, unreasonable, or even hostile attitudes of consumerists.

The writers of this sentence, and the many people who reviewed the brochure in draft form, knew what they wanted to say: that activists "misunderstand" or "lack understanding" of business operations. Instead, the double negative means that activists *do* understand—not the intent of the authors. Such misunderstandings lurk on and between the lines of all prose and need to be guarded against.

What the reader most needs must be most accessible to the reader.

Sometimes at the end of a project you are so familiar with the main point of your work, perhaps even bored by it, that you fail to communicate your point to the reader. You launch into the intriguing fine points rather than orienting the reader to what is important. Instead, think about what you want the reader to remember from your report and make that information easily accessible.

The rest of this guide expands on steps in the writing process within this framework of the communications model and writing to persuade readers. The last chapter shows how to shape the most common forms of professional writing: abstracts and executive summaries, memos, letters, proposals, reports, articles, and dissertations and theses.

Take time out from your writing to examine the process. Then, whether you're someone who loves to write and writes too much, or someone who hates to write, balks at the task, and perhaps is criticized for writing too little, you'll find here a way to make writing routine. It is that very routine that will help you write for results.

CONTEXT

Getting in Shape to Write

THE FIRST STEP in writing is to clarify the context for the memo, report, or proposal—whatever document is needed. Many hours of misdirected writing can be avoided if you think through the requirements for the document in advance of putting down line after line of prose on a yellow pad. In this chapter, we provide tools for defining the context around your writing. Once you know some specifics about who will read your work, what it should do, and what it should look like, then you can plan the writing efficiently and effectively, a topic we discuss in chapter 3. In chapter 4, we provide advice on the last step: putting words on paper.

Figure 2.1 provides an overview of the sub-steps in setting the context: assessing the assignment, defining the communications problem, and formulating the control statement. Let's look at each in detail.

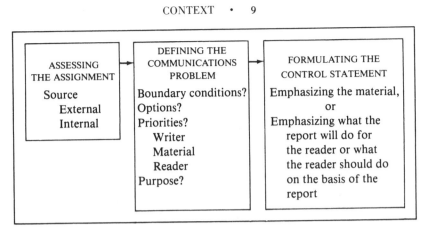

Figure 2.1
Setting the context for writing

Assessing the Assignment

All documents are the result of assignments. While there are as many assignments—as many reasons for writing—as there are documents, assignments fall into one of two types: external or internal. You write either because you are told to or because you want to. Happily, there are occasions on which you want to write what you are told to write.

The external assignment usually comes from someone higher in the organization than you: the vice-president of your division requests a report on the effect of the new travel policy on expenses; the manager of engineering asks for a status report on your research on the choice of material for a nosecone; the quality control supervisor wants an update on the relative merits of sewing and fusing linings for suitcoats.

The internal assignment is the one you impose on yourself: you identify a way to speed the flow of paper in your office and want to propose it to your supervisor; you decide to write an article for a professional journal on your research on nutritional standards for the elderly; you learn of a job opening in the company and write a letter of application.

One common mixed form of assignment is the response to an official *request for proposal* (RFP) or *request for quotation* (RFQ) issued by an industry or government agency. Here you are responding to an external request, but the decision to do so is yours.

Whether the assignment is imposed on you or by you, you have to *understand* it. Receiving an assignment is not always the same as understanding it. Especially when the assignment is given to you by someone else, you need to probe it carefully to be certain you know not just what is required but what is *not* required. If, for example, the quality control supervisor mentioned above requests the update on the relative merits of sewing and fusing of coat linings, be sure you know the limits: does he want to know what your firm is doing? Or does he want you to read the literature and make a few phone calls? When your assignment is to write a memo report, clarify the length desired and the time by which it is needed.

Try to answer these questions at the outset:

1. What form of document is called for?
2. What is the specific purpose of the document?
3. Who will read it?
4. When is it due?
5. What will the reader or readers do as a consequence of the document?
6. What do *you* want them to do?

The assignment itself, especially if it comes from someone else, may answer such questions directly. Or you may have to dig for answers. The digging should be part of a systematic approach to defining the communications problem.

Defining the Communications Problem

Defining the communications problem requires the same logical approach you use for defining a technical or professional problem. To define the problem, set forth the boundary conditions, options, priorities, and purpose for your writing. A careful assessment of these factors at the beginning of a writing project will speed your work and help assure a successful product.

BOUNDARY CONDITIONS

The first step in problem definition is to define the borders of the job. These boundary conditions may be specifically framed in the assignment. They may also be inherent in your materials or in your own skills.

The assignment may have directed you to focus on a particular incident—a failure at one of the company's generating stations—and specifically enjoined you from making generalizations about the operation of that type of generator elsewhere or from predicting other failures. The recipient of the report may set page limits: Robert S. Mc-Namara, at the Pentagon and at Ford, was well known for requiring that all memos sent to him be limited to one page each. The Department of Defense often sets page limits for contractor proposals. A journal or publisher sets standards for style—especially in organization, form of visuals, and presentation of references—for writing submitted to it. The management of a government agency or corporation may place security classifications on documents and thus limit what is presented. Your document may have to fit into a suitcoat pocket or meet the U.S. Postal Service specifications for mailing.

The material, too, may impose constraints. Some information is more easily presented in mathematics than in words, or in pictures than in mathematics. Sometimes, you have no material when you have to write, as in a monthly progress report at the end of a month in which nothing happened. Finally, your own skills are a limit on the kind of material you are able to discuss and your persuasiveness to the reader. You may have to seek a collaborator. You may have to build in more time than usual for writing when the work is particularly complex.

OPTIONS

Within the boundary conditions imposed on all projects you need to identify available options. Sometimes one option is not to communicate at all. Another may be to phone rather than write. In writing, you have available different forms— letters, memos, reports, books, articles, proposals, edited collections, and so on (see chapter 5). You may publish a set of instructions in a bound book; or you may use a three-ring notebook that eases updating when sections become obsolete. Within each form you have different possibilities for organization. You can start with the answer or build up to it. You can park all the technical details in an appendix or scatter them in the body of the report. You can use mostly pictures, or mostly numbers, or mostly words. You may shift emphasis away from what a project will cost to what it will achieve. Or you can emphasize cost. You can use your best jargon:

The relative possibility of our achieving an acceptable ratio of positive to negative evaluations on this contractual arrangement within the foreseeable future, given current exigencies, is probably best characterized as slim.

Or you can be direct:

We'll never win this contract.

PRIORITIES: WRITING FOR THE RECORD AND WRITING FOR READERS

Once you have determined the borders and options of the communications problem you are ready to establish priorities. Set priorities both for the *process* of writing—the tasks you'll perform—and for the *product* you hope to achieve. For the process, rank the writing among your other responsibilities and determine the amount of time and money it is worth.

For the product, the central priority is to determine if the writing is mainly for the record or mainly for the reader. Sometimes you write just to see how an idea looks on paper. You write to straighten out your own thinking. You write down notes on a meeting for your file or observations in the field or laboratory. You write for the record. As long as you can read and understand what you have written, then any options in form or language you select are fine. But when you introduce another reader (or readers) into the situation, then you must select from the options and conform to constraints to match the reader's needs. The reader's needs become a top priority.

To figure out the needs of your readers, try the three following methods, each shown in graphic form in figures 2.2, 2.3, and 2.4.

First, think of the reader as reflected in the *form* of writing you define as appropriate. Figure 2.2 arranges different forms on a scale from those meant mostly for the record to those shaped mostly by particular reader needs. A rise on the scale necessitates a shift from your own notes—which can be highly technical, in perhaps a private code, probably more visual than verbal—to writing which is overtly conscious of the reader. The language has to be more accessible. More interest-getting devices must be incorporated. Throughout this range, you must be aware of the balance between "incomprehensible accuracy" and "comprehensible inaccuracy," the poles one chemist and interpreter of sciences to nontechnical readers defined as the chief prob-

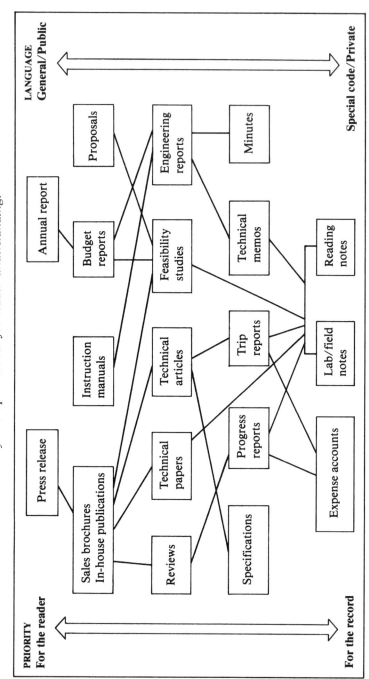

Figure 2.2

Documents arranged in levels according to priorities: writing for the record or writing for the reader. At the base, the material is most significant. A rise in level implies increasing attention to the reader's needs and special devices necessary to shape material for reader understanding.

PRIORITY
For the reader

LANGUAGE
General/Public

Special code/Private

For the record

Proposals

Engineering reports

Minutes

Annual report

Budget reports

Feasibility studies

Technical memos

Instruction manuals

Technical articles

Trip reports

Reading notes

Press release

Technical papers

Progress reports

Lab/field notes

Sales brochures
In-house publications

Reviews

Specifications

Expense accounts

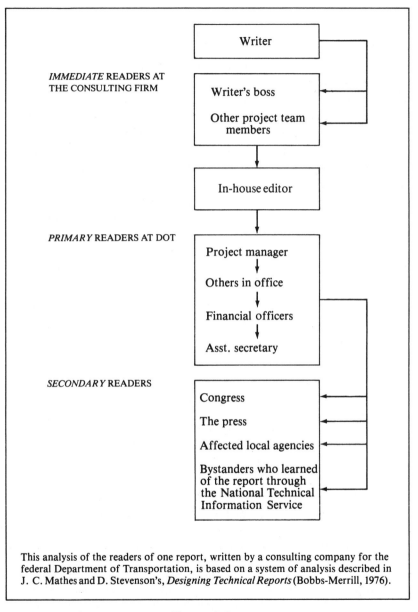

IMMEDIATE READERS AT
THE CONSULTING FIRM

Writer

Writer's boss

Other project team
members

In-house editor

PRIMARY READERS AT DOT

Project manager

Others in office

Financial officers

Asst. secretary

SECONDARY READERS

Congress

The press

Affected local agencies

Bystanders who learned
of the report through
the National Technical
Information Service

This analysis of the readers of one report, written by a consulting company for the federal Department of Transportation, is based on a system of analysis described in J. C. Mathes and D. Stevenson's, *Designing Technical Reports* (Bobbs-Merrill, 1976).

Figure 2.3
Chart of readers for the Philadelphia Area Transit Survey Report
(See pp. 98–101.)

lem in technical communication.[1] For the particular communications situation you are defining, determine the document's place on this scale.

Second, especially for a report intended for many readers, you might *plot the readers* on a chart like that shown in figure 2.3. This chart may also reflect the lines of communication that led to your assignment and that you now must report back through. The people on the chart may have contradictory needs. You'll have to determine the sequence of reading and the priorities among the readers to know whose needs must first be accommodated.

Third, determine from your analysis of the readers the *implications for writing* the document. Figure 2.4 provides answers to some key questions concerning readers.

To see some of these implications in action, read the following five passages. All concern the same material: the development of a new theory to explain color perception. Each is directed to a different set of readers. The examples are given here in order of decreasing technicality. The readership also broadens for each succeeding passage. If these were arranged on the scale in figure 2.2, they would move from the middle to the top, as shown in figure 2.5.

PASSAGE 1
"An External Point-Charge Model for Wavelength Regulation in Visual Pigments" by Barry Honig, Uri Dinur, Koji Nakanishi, Valeria Balough-Nair, Mary Ann Gawinowicz, Maria Arnaboldi, and Michael G. Motto.[2]

The chromophoric unit of visual pigments is known to consist of 11-*cis*-retinal covalently bound in the form of a protonated Schiff base to the c amino group of a lysine in the apoprotein opsin.[1] Protonated Schiff bases of retinal absorb at ~440 nm in

1. Edwin Slossen, as quoted by Robert H. Grant and Kenneth D. Fisher, "Scientists and Science Writers: Concerns and Proposed Solutions," *Federation Proceedings* (Federation of American Societies for Experimental Biology), 30 (1971), 819.

2. Reprinted with permission from the *Journal of the American Chemical Society*, 101 (1979): 7084. Copyright 1979 American Chemical Society.

QUESTION	ANSWER	IMPLICATIONS
Why is the audience reading this?	Has to, but isn't really interested.	Make it lively and brief; use introduction to attract interest.
	Will have to summarize its contents for someone higher up.	Write a clear, precise executive summary.
	Loves the topic and can't read enough on it.	Provide all the relevant details and don't hesitate to elaborate on interesting points.
What is the audience's level of technical understanding?	High — at least up to ours.	Don't hesitate to use specialized language; but don't over-explain.
	Low — lay audience.	Simplify discussions of technical matters; translate specialized language into English.
What can or will the audience do as a result of reading this?	Take some action.	Clearly focus on conclusions and recommended actions; say what should be done and why.
	File for reference.	Be sure all aspects of issues are covered adequately; don't worry about specific recommendations.
Are there any unique "political" implications you should be aware of?	Yes — sponsoring agency already did a study showing contradictory results.	Down-play differences between conclusions — but make your own clearly apparent.
	Yes — the sponsoring agency doesn't normally use the approach we did.	Make a special effort to explain why you chose the approach you did — its advantages, etc.
	Yes — Congress has expressed doubts about this project.	Give special attention to the secondary audience (Congress) and try to be especially persuasive.
	Yes — public opinion seems to be against this idea.	Write, for a lay audience, a well-developed defense or explanation of idea.

Figure 2.4
Writing implications of reader profile

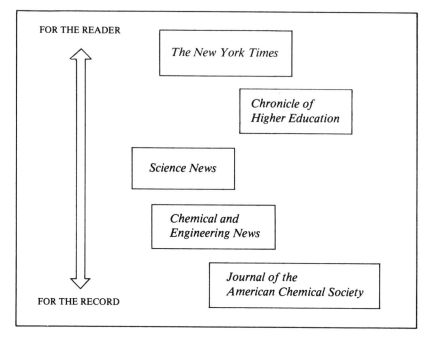

Figure 2.5
Passages on color vision arranged on chart of levels of documents

polar solvents while various salts formed in nonpolar solvents absorb at somewhat longer wavelength (~440–180 nm).[2] The visual pigment bovine rhodopsin has an absorption maximum of ~500 nm while other 11-*cis*-retinal-based visual pigments have maxima as far to the red as 580 nm. The mechanism through which the protein shifts the absorption maximum of the chromophore from its solution value to wavelengths ranging from 440 to 580 nm has been a question of major interest. In this communication we present the first experimentally based model which accounts for the absorption properties of a specific pigment, bovine rhodopsin.

This paragraph introduces a scientific correspondence. The authors, who are the scientists who did the work, assume that the reader is familiar with scientific terms (chromorphic unit, Schiff base, 11-*cis*-retinal). They begin directly with a discussion of what is known as a way of introducing the question of what has not been known—the mechanism of absorption. Then they state that their article presents the first experimentally based model for the mechanism. The discussion is detailed. Several modifiers are stacked up tightly against nouns: "other 11-*cis*-retinal-based visual pigments." The authors use technical terms to achieve precision and accuracy. They refer to the literature (superscripts 1 and 2).

PASSAGE 2

"Chemical Model for Color Vision Resolved: Precisely located external charges, likely arising from attached proteins, enable 11-*cis*-retinal to transmit color signals to the brain" by Jeffrey L. Fox.[3]

A single molecule, that by itself has sensitivity to ultraviolet light, serves the eye by providing sensitivity to the broad spectrum of visible light. The way that the molecule, 11-*cis*-retinal, presents the brain with a rainbow instead of mere shadowy images now has yielded to precise chemical explanation.

The effort to develop that explanation "took many years" and involved about a dozen scientists, principal among them organic chemist Koji Nakanishi of Columbia University in New York City and biophysicist Barry Honig now at the University of Illinois, Urbana. The project has depended on the synthesis of a family of highly unstable compounds closely related to 11-*cis*-retinal and subsequent analysis showing how that one compound can serve several biochemical masters to give broad spectrum visual perception.

As its title implies, *Chemical and Engineering News (C&EN)* appeals to both scientific and technical people. The author of this introductory passage is a staff writer, not the researchers. The article begins with an explanation, more concrete than theoretical and including definitions, of light sensitivity. The name of the molecule (11-*cis*-retinal) is given, but defined as new information the reader is not assumed to know. The author concentrates on the news aspects of the researchers rather than just their findings. The

3. Reprinted with permission from *Chemical and Engineering News*, Nov. 12, 1979, p. 25. Copyright 1979 American Chemical Society.

first paragraph also sets up a sense of mystery that leads the reader into the second. The paragraphs are shorter than in the first example; this structure eases reading. The article's title draws attention and gives the answer.

PASSAGE 3
"Color vision: A matter of charge." From *Science News*, Dec. 22 and 29, 1979, p. 427.[4]

Each light-sensitive cell of the human eye responds to a particular wavelength of light. Some sense red, some green and others blue. Yet the same chemical component is involved in detecting each hue. A molecule called 11-*cis*-retinal absorbs light in every receptor cell, but the large protein molecule to which the retinal is bound determines what wavelength of light it best absorbs. Now Koji Nakanishi of Columbia University and Barry Honig of the University of Illinois report just how the protein influences retinal's light absorption. Precisely located negative charges, probably on the amino acids of the proteins, are responsible for color discrimination.

Science News is a popular publication with a circulation of 170,000. This introduction, like that in *C&EN*, begins with an explanation of color vision, but in even more concrete and simple terms. It introduces 11-*cis*-retinal slowly, with background first. More transitional words (*yet, but, now*) are used to guide the reader. The sense of the new is also exploited: "Now [the researchers] report just how. . . ." A brief overview of the mechanism is given in the last sentence, so that a reader interested only in the mechanism in general could stop there.

PASSAGE 4
"Color-vision explained." From *The Chronicle of Higher Education*, Dec. 10, 1979, p. 6.[5]

4. Reprinted with permission from *Science News*, the weekly magazine of science, copyright 1979 by Science Service, Inc.
5. Appeared originally in *The Chronicle of Higher Education*, Dec. 10, 1979. Reprinted with permission. Copyright 1979 by The Chronicle of Higher Education, Inc.

How and why human beings, monkeys, freshwater fish, and a few other animals see colors has been explained for the first time by Koji Nakanishi, an organic chemist at Columbia University.

For years, scientists have known that the body gets "11-*cis*-retinal," a light-absorbing molecule that governs perception of color, from fish and dark green vegetables that contain vitamin A. Once absorbed into the body, the vitamin-A derivative travels to the eye's retina, where it binds with one of four "visual proteins," known more commonly as pigments, three of which are involved in color vision.

The *Chronicle*, with a circulation of 68,000, is read mainly by university administrators and faculty from all disciplines, not particularly those in science. So the author can't assume that the readers are motivated to read about this topic. Motivation must be built in. To do this, the author moves to the level of the picturable and familiar—human beings, monkeys, freshwater fish—away from the level of molecules and protons. The author also stresses the news value—"for the first time"—but stresses only the principal investigator, Nakanishi. The names of the researchers are also generalized as we move to more broadly popular accounts. Note how the technical terms here are in quotation marks, the author's acknowledgment that the reader is not familiar with them. More definitions are given. The language and approach are straightforward.

PASSAGE 5

"Scientists Discover Answer to Color Perception by Eye" by Dava Sobel. From the *New York Times*, Nov. 28, 1979, p. A20.[6]

Working with highly sensitive chemicals in a red-lit laboratory at near-freezing temperatures scientists at Columbia University have performed experiments enabling them to answer a hundred-year-old question about color vision.

Their new understanding of normal color perception may also

6. Copyright 1979 by The New York Times Company. Reprinted by permission.

point the way to future practical applications in the treatment of color blindness.

Prof. Koji Nakanishi and his collaborators have demonstrated how a single substance, called retinal, can be responsible for perception of all four types of color messages: red, green, blue, and black and white.

In the *Times* account, emphasis shifts from the research to the researchers, and particularly those at a local institution, Columbia University. The tale is told as a story of happenings in a "red-lit laboratory," at "near-freezing temperatures." The reader is motivated to read by the drama and sense of discovery in research ("to answer a hundred-year-old-question"). Practical applications are also stressed— applications are not mentioned in the other passages. These answer the reader's question of "What's in it for me or anyone not in science?" Note that the substance has here been generalized to the term "retinal," an effect of the need perhaps for "comprehensible inaccuracy." But this audience doesn't require more precision in naming. Paragraphs are short—one sentence each—to keep the reader's eye moving.

PURPOSE

Each of the above passages differs in the devices used to tailor material to a different audience. Different readers' needs shape each document. The passages share a common purpose: to inform. At the same time, one can find other purposes operating. In the *ACS* journal, for example, a purpose of the researchers in writing is to establish their claim to the *first* explanation. The *Times* article aims to entertain while it informs. The *Chronicle* shows university people what two university people have done. Each of these articles conforms to some well-defined purposes.

In defining your communications problem, you too need to assess your purpose—what you want to accomplish in writing, some measurable outcome of your work. Such objectives parallel—but are not the same as—the objectives for your professional activity. The purpose is usually defined in terms of the *reader* or of the *material*. In a letter, the purpose might be what you want the *reader* to do when he or she has finished it. File it? Then your purpose is mainly to document an activity. The text should be detailed and technical, providing answers to any questions that may be raised later on. Respond to it? Then you need to be persuasive, to show how the reader, too, may benefit. To a degree determined by the needs of the reader, you should place less emphasis on what you have done, and more on what the reader ought to do. Whenever possible, go into a huddle with the reader before you write to agree on the purpose.

You may also define your purpose in terms of your *material*. You want to display your information in the best possible light, to achieve the best advantage from it. If the objective is comprehensiveness, as in a dissertation (see chapter 5), then elaboration on the state-of-the-art, detailed tables and charts of laboratory experiments, extended narrative of method, and complete calculations may be required. But one of the problems people face in turning dissertations into articles and books is a shift in the purpose of communication: comprehensiveness becomes less appropriate than innovation. A new objective might be to show what is unique in your material, in the results you achieved, or in the method you developed. A clear understanding of purpose gives you the momentum necessary to shift from analyzing and defining the problem to writing an effective and efficient report.

Formulating the Control Statement

In defining the problem, then, you simply explore who will read your work, what it should do, and what it should look like. You narrow the options to see what form, organization, and language will be appropriate. Right from the beginning, discuss with everyone concerned not only the substance of your professional task, but also the means of expressing that substance to those who will use your findings. Clearly understanding the communications problem leads you to the last step in setting the context: formulating the control statement. This statement is a one-sentence summary of the content of your report, article, letter, memo—whatever. Until you can say what your document is all about in one sentence, you're not ready to write. In this statement, you turn from assessing the problem to structuring the document that will solve the problem. The statement gives you a track to run on. Writing a control statement is both tricky and engaging. But once such a statement is well crafted, you're on your way to a good report.

In composing the control statement, you can look back to your *material* to see what all your work adds up to. Or you can look forward to the *document*, to see what the document should do for the reader. One kind of control statement emphasizes the material. It may state a fact, perhaps, as in a sales document, emphasizing a benefit:

The alumni fund's special project solicitation has reached this year's goal of $4 million and is already ahead on projected receipts for the first two months of the new year.

The report details the receipt of gifts, including information about why that goal was set and who made major donations. It then describes projections for the new year and current status.

The control statement may also be a generalization:

The forms of financial services are constantly changing in response to social, economic, and technological forces.

After a brief introduction to the "forms," this report describes changes in each of the three categories in the order given: social, economic, and technological. The generalization is thus proven.

In this communication we present the first experimentally based model which accounts for the absorption of a specific pigment, bovine rhodopsin.

A single molecule, that by itself has sensitivity to ultraviolet light, serves the eye by providing sensitivity to the broad spectrum of visible lights.

These control statements summarize the material. They state what the author finds significant in the work.

Another way to look at formulating the statement is to think about the role of the document in the life of the reader. What do you want your reader to do when he or she finishes reading? What have *you* done for the reader? How should the reader read the report? The statement answers some of these questions.

I am again writing to ask you to dig down and invest in a scholar of the future.

This sentence—a variant on a familiar theme—begins a solicitation for the alumni fund. On a less pressing note, here's another reader-oriented statement:

This report presents a series of projections of barge traffic flow on the Ohio River system through 1990 to assist the U.S. Army Corps of Engineers in planning the construction and maintenance of the locks and dams that make the system navigable.

The report describes the projections in terms appropriate for Corps planning.

One caution: it is easy to confuse your research objective with your communications objective, as can be seen in the following:

· The purpose of this report is to investigate the need for dietary iron of women in their childbearing years.

The above sentence gives the purpose of the *research* rather than the *report*. Based on the research, the final report might have one (or more) of the following *purposes:*

- This report recommends a federal program to distribute to women of childbearing age information about their special need for dietary iron.
- This report reviews the literature written since 1975 on the need for dietary iron among women of childbearing age.
- This report summarizes a two-year study sponsored by the National Institute of Medicine concerning the optimal levels of dietary iron intake in females between 14 and 42 years of age.

The initial confusion between the purpose of the professional activity and the purpose of the communications activity may cause a misdirection of the final report.

In one document, you may have a control statement that emphasizes the material, or one that emphasizes the reader. Or you may mix these. It's simply important to sit back at the end of the problem-definition stage and think about what your work adds up to. This sum is not merely a topic,

the small-scale modeling technique

but a sentence that ties the topic down to some action:

The purpose of this report is to demonstrate the validity of direct, small-scale modeling techniques, already established in studies of cast-in-place concrete structures, for studies of large-panel, precast industrialized building systems.

The rest of your writing is merely a setting forth of the implications of this sentence. The sentence predicts both the content and the form of your report. It governs the admission of evidence. It heads you in a direction to maintain the reader's interest. With the sentence in hand, you are ready to plan the document the control statement promises.

The Context Defined

In establishing the context, then:

1. Assess the assignment.

2. Define the communications problem:

What *boundary conditions* constrain the writing?
What are my *options* in writing?
What are my *priorities* for the document?
 Am I writing mainly for the record or for the reader?
 If for a reader, who?
 What are the reader's needs and level of understanding?
 What is most important in my material, my work?
 How can I present the work to my best advantage?
What is my final *purpose*—my objective—in writing?

3. Formulate the control statement:

It may emphasize the *material:*
 This is a report about. . . .
It may emphasize the *reader:*
 The purpose of this [fill in the name of the document: memo, letter, report, . . .] for [fill in the name of the recipient] is to . . . [fill in the purpose: recommend, report, describe, . . .].

· 3 ·

PLANNING

From Analysis to Design

IN DEFINING the communications problem, you analyzed the environment for your document and assessed the potential of your material and the expectations of whatever readers you need to address. The result of this analysis is a control statement. What does that statement control? It controls the admission of evidence into the document and the sequencing of that information: what goes in and in what order.

The first stage of writing is analysis. The second stage is design. You find out first what is needed: the assignment and its implications. Then you design the document that will solve the problem. Designing the document really means expanding the control statement, breaking out the parts of the statement that will form the major divisions of the document (figure 3.1).

Of course, turning the corner from analysis to design is not irreversible. During your analysis, you might jot down some notes on a plan for a section. While you're planning, you might need to look back at part of the problem that has not been well defined. Certain key features of planning set this step apart. You turn from gathering material to deploying it. You set up the terms of your information brokering. You establish a communications program, a plan of attack on the communications problem.

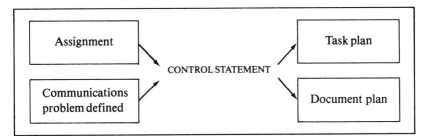

Figure 3.1
From analysis to design

The program really consists of two plans: a plan of the *tasks* in writing and a plan of the *document* that will result. Their formality and elaborateness depend on the length and difficulty of the document to be planned, the number of people to be coordinated in writing, and the number of required preliminary reviews and approvals. The two plans can be compared this way:

Task plan	*Document plan*
Shapes the activities that lead to the document	Shapes the final document
Controls persons and actions	Controls contents of document
Is developed from managerial analysis of needs and resources	Is developed from control statement
Serves as a timetable to guide actions of writers, editors, production personnel	Serves as a checklist to evaluate success of document in meeting needs of readers

Task Plan

PURPOSE

To plan the tasks associated with writing, answer questions like these:

· What is to be done?
· For whom is it to be done?
· Why is it to be done?
· When is it to be done?
· Who is to do it?

Then, based on the answers, define the steps to prepare for writing and place these on a time line. Be particularly careful about *deadlines* and *coordination of contributors.*

Establishing deadlines gives you a framework for everything else. Make sure the receiver of your communication agrees on the deadlines. Set your own deadlines in advance of public ones to allow for contingencies. Set preliminary deadlines for steps in a large project.

If you're writing alone, you can note a target completion date on your desk calendar and pace yourself to meet it. If, however, you are responsible for coordinating the work of others, then you may need a more formal setting forth of answers to questions about the context and deadlines. Share your definition of the communications problem with the team, in either a meeting or a memo. Show how each person's contribution is shaped by the purpose of the document. Make clear to team members how their work is interrelated. Serve as liaison to the person to whom the final project is to be submitted and schedule checks on its progress with him or her. Allow time for necessary reviews and approvals as well as the mechanics of final assembly, production, and shipping.

FORM

The task plan may exist simply as a note to yourself; or, for larger projects, you may describe the schedule for writing in a form parallel to the schedule for other managerial tasks. Figure 3.2 shows a Gantt chart, a form of a table that may be used to show simultaneous and sequential activities over time. The line for each activity can then be filled in as the task is completed to display progress on the project. Such a

TASKS	WEEKS									
	1	2	3	4	5	6	7	8	9	10
Preliminary discussion	▪									
Assignment of tasks	▪									
Information gathering	▬	▬								
Circulation of summary and preliminary outline			▬							
Meeting on outline to plan draft					▪					
Writing						▬				
Collection and review of drafts							▬			
Preparation of visuals								▬		
Editing									▪	
Production										▬

Figure 3.2
Gantt chart for a multiple-author document

chart attached to the coordinator's wall provides immediate reminders of how the writing is progressing.

Document Plan

PURPOSE

The task plan controls your activities as a writer. The document plan controls the design of the final document. It matches the boundary conditions, options, priorities, and purpose you have established for the document. The plan offers several benefits:

• allows you to see how the final document will look before you encase it in prose
• allows you to test alternative patterns for lining up material
• subordinates the details of the material
• fosters coherence and emphasis
• assures that evidence is appropriately ordered to support the control statement
• provides a track to run on when you write.

PATTERNS FOR PRESENTATION

The process of planning is an exercise in distributing material to the right place and the right method of presentation. Information is different—has different impact and meaning—in different settings. The patterns for sequencing information are classifiable into three orders: natural, logical, and psychological. Within a document, certain kinds of information also belong in the introduction, other kinds in the body, and others in the ending. And some information is best expressed verbally, some visually, and some mathematically. Here is some advice on deciding how to arrange your information.

The Three Orders

One way to decide about sequencing information is to think in terms of three fundamental orders:

• *natural order,* imposed by the material
• *logical order,* imposed by the writer
• *psychological order,* imposed by the reader

Natural order is determined by the material. It can be either spatial or chronological. Spatial order is, simply, the order of space: from right to left, top to bottom, east to west. A description of the terrain of a building site can follow spatial order, as can that of a building, machine, or any other physical item. Chronological order is the order of time: from then to now, year to year, day to day, minute to minute. Reviews of literature often follow chronological order, from the first publication on a topic to the latest. A report of a laboratory experiment is also often chronological in that it begins with the setting up of the test and follows through to the results.

Logical order is determined by the writer, who imposes the order on the material. There are many useful subtypes:

• *Pro and con, and comparison-contrast:* All arguments for are gathered at one place, and all arguments against are gathered at another.
• *General-to-specific and specific-to-general:* Start with the central observation and then enumerate the illustrative details, or build up the details and then present the observation that grows out of them.
• *Classification:* Group discrete items under appropriate headings (small and large, toxic and nontoxic, expenses and revenues, blue and red).

There are of course other versions of logical order. You, the writer, put bounds on the material, forcing it into groups, laying out the pattern.

Psychological order derives from the writer's awareness of the reader's needs. This form of development requires you to arrange information particularly to please the reader. If the reader is primarily concerned with cost and only secondarily interested in the technical details, then psychological order obligates you to present the financial information first and most accessibly, subordinating the technical details even though you happen to consider them more interesting.

The following three paragraphs illustrate the ways in which the choice of order affects the presentation of the same information. These are reviews of the performance of the Consumer Products Division of the Webfoot Corporation during the second quarter of 1982.

NATURAL—CHRONOLOGICAL

Sales in April were unusually strong, probably the result of severe weather in the Midwest that increased demand for our storm-alert systems. We recorded sales of $37 million that month, and inventories dropped to just under $100 million. Earnings on sales remained at their March level of 7 percent. May sales dipped to $25 million, while earnings as a percent of sales and inventories remained at April levels. In June, earnings improved, rising to 9 percent of sales, partly as a result of careful cost controls implemented in our Birmingham plant. Sales returned to their April level of $37 million, and inventories increased to $110 million because of a planned speed-up at the North Berwyn plant.

LOGICAL—CLASSIFICATION AND EXPLANATION

During the second quarter, sales amounted to $99 million. Earnings for the period were $7.9 million, or 8 percent of sales. Inventories increased over the period from $100 million at the beginning of April to $110 million at the end of June. Severe weather in the Midwest contributed to good sales early in the quarter; the cost-control system in effect in the Birmingham plant improved productivity there, while a planned speed-up at the North Berwyn facility increased output and added to the inventory build-up.

PSYCHOLOGICAL

Sales and earnings achieved projections once again in the second quarter. Sales nearly reached the $100 million mark. Earnings for the period were $7.9 million; margins improved substantially over the period, moving from 7 to 9 percent, a tribute to the cost-control system introduced at the Birmingham plant. Production is also improving significantly and according to plan at the North Berwyn plant.

The first paragraph arranges information month by month. All information about storms and sales is presented at the same level of emphasis, riding along a time line. The second paragraph follows a pattern of classification and explanation. First, information on total sales, earnings, and inventories is summarized; that result is then explained. The third paragraph aims to please and convince the reader by announcing items of good news. First it reports that the division "achieved projections once again," and then it lists components of this success. Each positive factor is supported by a reference to the work of particular divisions. The weather is omitted.

Introduction, Body, Ending

The three orders may at times overlap. All may be used effectively in a single document. Where? Any communication, oral or written, has three discrete parts: introduction, body, and ending. In long documents, you may add a fourth, the appendix, which contains supporting information that need not appear in the body but that should be available for reference. The introduction and ending usually require special attention to the reader's needs, which means that psychological order is called for. They are the bridges over which you conduct the reader into and out of the document. To set up and finish the body of a document, you'll probably require logical order. In the middle, the heart of the discussion, natural order may prevail. The introduction orients the reader to the subject, provides context and background, gives an overview, and in general interests the reader and prepares him or her for what is to follow. The body is the substantive core of the paper or presentation—the facts, interpretations, and discussion. The ending debriefs; it pulls together the key features of the body and puts them in summary form for the reader. It often includes either or both conclusions (the main points) and recommendations (suggestions on what to do about these main points). The introduction and ending are thus both highly *reader*-oriented, while the body is *material*-oriented.

The job of planning is to distribute the information at hand into one (or sometimes several) of these four parts. Knowing what to put where is the key. Here are a few guidelines on distribution:

1.   The most general information belongs in the introduction. Quotations attesting to the significance of the topic, statements about the relation of the subject to a larger con-

text, and overviews all constitute introductory material. The control statement belongs here. So also do conclusions, unless the author has a valid reason for withholding them, like an anticipated reader objection.

2. Technical information belongs in the body. (Highly technical matter might go in the appendix if its appearance in the body proper is not necessary.) Statistics, lab results, observations, and interpretations drawn from the literature comprise the body of the document—its core.

3. Summary information belongs in the ending. The ending should not introduce a new topic, but may look to future implications of the topic at hand. It brings the reader out of the welter of details and highlights what should be remembered from the report.

Verbal and Visual Methods of Presentation

In addition to choosing a pattern of development in the planning stage, you should select the appropriate method of presentation: verbal, visual, or mathematical. Discursive prose is sometimes the least efficient means of information transfer. Many writers and readers think more effectively in images or numbers than in words. These needs must be accommodated. Making a preliminary choice in the planning phase about whether to use verbal, visual, or mathematical presentation helps you sort out the tasks better and gives you greater flexibility. You can determine just what writing has to be done and what tables, graphs, or charts must be prepared.

What material should be presented visually? There are some obvious answers. A discussion of the political constraints on the development of nuclear power requires prose. No table can do full justice to the subtleties of that topic. On the other hand, prose is inefficient as a way of presenting the financial position of a corporation. Instead, a balance sheet (basically a visual form incorporating words and numbers) does that job directly and easily.

Sometimes, of course, both verbal and visual methods are needed. It is simply not true that "the numbers speak for themselves." Words are often required to explain those numbers. Hence an annual report includes not just financial statements but management's discussion of them. An excellent point can easily be lost if it is made only on a graph, but by the same token a set of lab results pointing to a clear conclusion about the behavior of a fiber probably cannot be presented exclusively in sentences.

In choosing a method of presentation, consider characteristics of the information, reader, and writer.

CHARACTERISTICS OF THE INFORMATION Keep the following basic points in mind.

Visual: Inherently visual material should be presented visually. If a floor plan is a necessary part of the report, don't try to capture it exclusively in a written description. Present the plan itself as a figure, and then provide whatever verbal highlighting is required. If the material to be presented *is* a picture, include it that way unless the method or cost of reproduction, or another constraint, prohibits.

Numerical: Numbers should be presented as numbers. The market share of a product over time takes the form of numbers; you surely want to comment verbally on the significance, but don't substitute words for the numbers themselves.

Verbal: Concepts that are primarily verbal should be presented in sentences. While visual or numerical forms may help to make a point, there is really no alternative to a verbal description of an abstract term like "fiduciary" or "black hole."

CHARACTERISTICS OF THE READER As mentioned, some people are simply more visually than verbally oriented, or more numerical than visual. In choosing a method of presentation, try to accommodate the reader's need and play to his or her strengths. An accountant almost always responds more quickly to—and grasps more fully—a numerical presentation, whereas a general manager ordinarily prefers a verbal description of a problem. Architects and city planners are highly visual and therefore are better served by plans, sections, and views, than by tables. Engineers and scientists often think in graphs and tables, which makes those forms appropriate for them.

Levels of sophistication or familiarity in the reader require different approaches. For a popular audience, visual displays can be helpful in making complex issues concrete and understandable. On the day after the President submits his annual budget to Congress, every newspaper in America provides a pie chart showing the distribution of income and expenses. Why? Because that simple—though perhaps overworked—form quickly distills the complexities of the budget into an easily grasped image. Everyone understands the division of a pie.

CHARACTERISTICS OF THE WRITER   In selecting a form of presentation, you should consider your own temperament and skills as well as the characteristics of the material and the reader. If you think visually rather than verbally, you should consider presenting your information visually. You're probably better at it. If numbers excite you, use tables and equations. If you never did understand Gantt charts but can crystalize the meaning of a production schedule in a few deft sentences, then by all means write the description and avoid the chart. Within the obvious constraints of the material and the reader's needs, play to your own strengths.

Good prose—and good communication generally—always aims at a balance of details and generalizations. In choosing appropriate methods of presentation, follow the principle of balance. When details appear to overwhelm a verbal discussion it's a hint to you that the mix is supersaturated, that you should precipitate out some of the details into nonverbal forms. Dense prose can be loosened when details are removed and placed in tables, graphs, or other visual or numerical forms of presentation. Striking the right balance between details and generalizations is often made easier by the use of a mix of verbal and nonverbal forms of presentation.

FORM OF THE DOCUMENT PLAN

The plan results from a series of decisions about where and how information should appear in a document. The plan is your tool, so its form should be one that is comfortable. Some people use traditional outlines, with Roman numerals for main headings:

I.
  A.
    1.
    2.
  B.
II.

Others, especially those geared to the military, use a numbered outline:

1.0
  1.1
    1.1.1
    1.1.2
  1.2
2.0

These are linear plans. They are models of the final product. Other writers prefer nonlinear planning devices that follow the direction of the writer's thinking in honing in on the problem. They are models of the *process* of writing. Nonlinear planning often precedes a linear plan for the document. Few people think linearly, but that's the only way a document makes sense: readers proceed from sentence one to sentence two. The process of thinking is more random. Here are some suggestions concerning forms for both nonlinear and linear planning.

Nonlinear Plans

One way to begin the plan is with a "data dump." Figure 3.3 shows the data dump for some writing about the supplemental benefits package of a hypothetical firm, Smurf, Inc. On a large sheet of paper, the author simply wrote down

- Blue Cross / Blue Shield, full individual coverage paid for by company ($950/year), company contributes 80% of amount over individual (1 additional = $600, family = $900)
- Health Maintenance Organizations available:
  Los Angeles Health Plan (company cost = $1000/individual)
  California Health Plan ($900)
  Southern California Health Maintenance Organization ($1100)
- Life insurance (group life) 2 × salary paid for by company
- Dental coverage (available after 6 mos. employment; individual coverage $280, family $425)
  first year, company pays 50% — employee pays 50%
  second year   75   25
  third year   100%
- Long term disability insurance in effect after 6 months of employment
- FICA
- Stock purchase plan after one year of employment — employee can contribute up to 5% of gross salary — company matches contribution toward purchase of company's stock without brokerage commission
- 8 paid holidays a year + 3 personal days + vacations — 1 week on joining company, after 1 year, 2 weeks; 5 years, 3 weeks; 9 years, 4 weeks
- Tuition plan — after 1 year, company pays 75% of tuition and books at accredited college to take appropriate degree or other course (who decides?)
- Retirement plan — join after one year, have to join after 5 years, 5% contribution from employee matched by 5% from company, fully vested
- Membership in company management club and use of lodge with golf course

Figure 3.3

Data dump. Information (in this case, about a company's benefits package) is randomly "dumped" on a large sheet of paper. No order is imposed. The writer simply jots down items as they come to mind along with any questions the items spark that the writer wants to investigate.

notes on the material as ideas came. He imposed no order, but let his initial ideas engender others. The context for writing remained in the back of the writer's mind as a screen, but otherwise he just wrote. The writer kept the sheet on a bulletin board for a few days and added notes as the ideas came.

As a step toward order, once he had flushed out the topics he wanted to cover, he classified the items (figure 3.4) by circling and drawing lines to related items. Figure 3.5 shows the information classified into sets—another method of ordering.

These approaches might be called "bottom up planning." The author started with a jumble of details. Such planning can be conducted at a blackboard rather than on a sheet of paper. Especially in a group writing project, a session with the coordinator at the board can be helpful. Each contributor suggests pertinent topics. The topics are recorded and then classified. The coordinator screens topics as they are suggested for pertinence to the document. Another variant is to jot topics on slips of paper, then arrange these on a bulletin board in a variety of orders.

Other approaches may be called "top down planning." You may skip the data dump and proceed directly to lining up material. Figure 3.6 shows a branching of topics under key terms. The lines indicate cross-referencing among items that support more than one term. Given an understanding of some general patterns of organization, you may proceed directly to shaping material in one pattern. Figure 3.7 shows information scheduled chronologically. This table may be read down (to determine the benefits available in a given year) or across (to follow the path of a particular benefit over time).

The order of presentation may also be set by the reader as part of the assignment. The request for a proposal may, in effect, become the outline for your response. The same is true of military specifications for defense contractor bids, proposals, and reports. You may be given either headings or questions that must be answered in a preset order. The request structures your work.

Blue Cross / Blue Shield, full individual coverage
paid for by company ($950/year), company
contributes 80% of amount over individual (1
additional = $600, family = $900)

Health Maintenance Organizations available:
Los Angeles Health Plan (company cost =
$1000/individual)
California Health Plan ($900)
Southern California Health Maintenance
Organization ($1100)

health insurance

Life insurance (group life) 2 × salary paid
for by company

Dental coverage (available after 6 mos. employment;
individual coverage $280, family $425)
first year, company pays 50% — employee pays 50%
second year   75   25
third year   100%

Long term disability insurance in effect after 6
months of employment

FICA

Stock purchase plan after one year of employment
— employee can contribute up to 5% of gross
salary — company matches contribution
toward purchase of company's stock without
brokerage commission

other

8 paid holidays a year + 3 personal days +
vacations — 1 week on joining company, after
1 year, 2 weeks; 5 years, 3 weeks; 9 years,
4 weeks

vacation

Tuition plan — after 1 year, company pays 75%
of tuition and books at accredited college to
take appropriate degree or other course
(who decides?)

Retirement plan — join after one year, have to
join after 5 years, 5% contribution from
employee matched by 5% from company,
fully vested

retirement

Membership in company management club and
use of lodge with golf course

Figure 3.4
The data dump classified

You may also begin with the control statement, then deploy information in support. Each word in the statement must be backed. Two examples of this are shown in figure 3.8.

The blueprint for the entire document appears on one

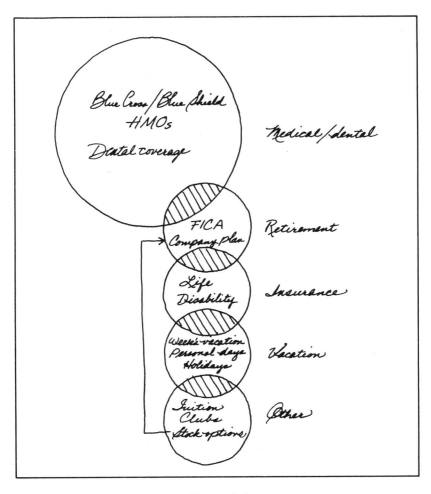

Figure 3.5
Information classified into sets. Hatched areas represent overlaps in categories. Arrows indicate cross-references (items that can belong in more than one set).

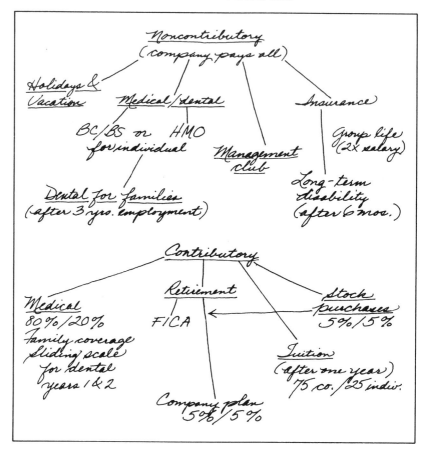

Figure 3.6
*A branching of topics from key words. Here, the purpose of the classifica-
tion is to arrange the benefits into two large categories: those that are free
to employees and those to which the employees contribute.*

side of one sheet of paper (see figure 3.8). The statement is
the target, written in bold letters at the top as a constant
reminder to the writer. Three columns are lined off. The
basic sections—introduction, body, ending, and appendix—are sketched in. Once the form is set, you can
begin jotting anywhere on it you like—you don't need to
begin with the introduction. It's probably best to begin at

Figure 3.7

A chronological sequencing of items. In this organization, the benefits are lined up according to the year of employment with the company in which the employee begins to participate. Categories are parallel from year to year.

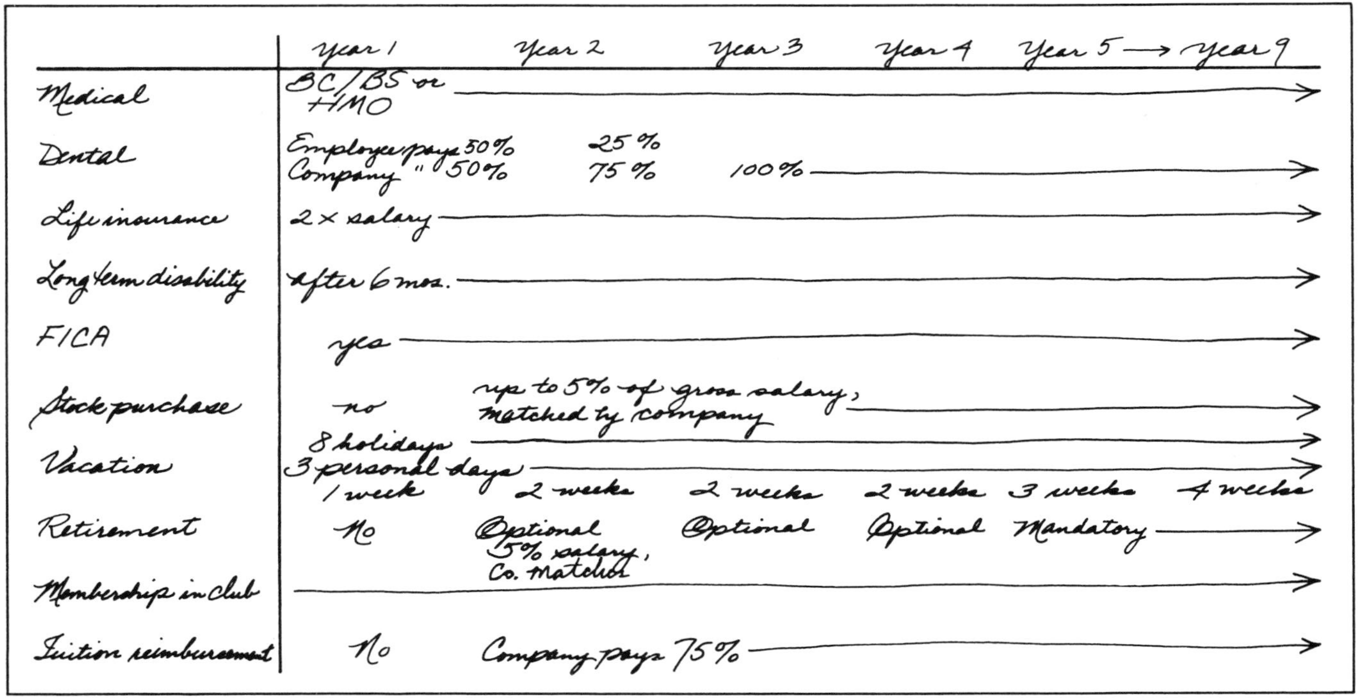

	Year 1	Year 2	Year 3	Year 4	Year 5 → Year 9
Medical	BC/BS or HMO →				
Dental	Employee pays 50% Company " 50%	25% 75%	100% →		
Life insurance	2× salary →				
Long term disability	after 6 mos. →				
FICA	yes →				
Stock purchase	no	up to 5% of gross salary Matched by company →			
Vacation	8 holidays 3 personal days 1 week	2 weeks	2 weeks	2 weeks 3 weeks	4 weeks →
Retirement	No	Optional 5% salary, Co. matched	Optional	Optional Mandatory	→
Membership in club				Mandatory →	
Tuition reimbursement	No	Company Pays 75% →			

Figure 3.8
Two large sheet outlines. In (A), the benefits package is presented in a brochure to orient new employees. In (B), the same general information is tailored for a report from the Human Resources Development Department of the company to the company president.

A) Control statement: Smurf, Inc., offers its employees an excellent benefits package that is carefully designed to provide needed protection and to extend compensation in tax-shielded ways.

INTRO	BODY	FIG	CONCLUSIONS
Comprehensive package of— • traditional (health, dental, life, disability, FICA, retirement, vacation & holidays) • special (stock purchase, management club, tuition) Designed to— • help meet emergencies, etc. • supplement direct comp with tax-shielded benefits	*Traditional* 1. Health (BC/BS; 3 HMOs) 2. Life (2 × salary) 3. Dental 4. Disability 5. Retirement (FICA, company plan) 6. Vacations & holidays *Special* 1. Stock purchase 2. Tuition 3. Managment club	1 2	Comprehensive package to meet employee needs & provide added compensation APPENDIX Full descriptions of plans, costs eligibility, etc.

B) Control statement: Smurf, Inc., offers a competitive benefits package designed to maintain employee morale, reduce turnover, reward longevity, and control costs.

INTRO	BODY	FIG	CONCLUSIONS
Our benefits package is — • Competitive • Important in maintaining employee morale and productivity & reducing turnover • Carefully controlled to avoid abuse (esp. through length-of-service limitations) • Cost effective	*Schedule of benefits & costs* (details in appendix) • Total cost to Smurf: $7,917,708 • Average cost/employee, $6,522 • 32.6% of direct salaries *Length-of-service limitations* Dental (6 mos.) Disability (6 mos.) Stock purchase (1 yr.) Tuition (1 yr.) Co. retirement (1 yr.) Vacations (varies) *Employee contributions* Health (family) Stock purchase Dental (increasing co. participation) Tuition Co. retirement	1 2 3	Reiterate main pts. of intro., stressing fit of package to goals of productivity, morale, loyalty, cost control, etc. APPENDIX Yearly cost to Smurf, Inc.: | Benefit	Avg. cost per employee	Total	 |---|---|---| | Health	$1420	$1,723,880	 | Dental	425	515,950	 | Life premiums	289	350,846	 | Disability	73	88,622	 | FICA	1800	2,185,200	 | Stock/match	380	461,320	 | Tuition	270	327,780	 | Co. retirement	800	971,200	 | Mgmt. club	80	97,120	 | Vac., holidays	985	1,195,790	 | Total	$6,522	$7,917,708	 1214 employees Direct salaries, $24,280,000 Benefits 32.6% of salaries

the appendix and see what you can park there to streamline the discussion. You can check easily for emphasis and digressions. You can check for omissions. You can also indicate along the right side of each column where you want to include visuals, a decision to be made at the planning stage. You can work on the plan nonlinearly; but once completed, the outline in this form becomes a linear plan you can follow to write the document. Each of the main topics becomes a heading in the text. Physical relationships among sections in the plan stand for logical relationships in the material.

Linear Plans

The large sheet plans in figure 3.8 convert the nonlinear process into the beginnings of linear plans. You may write directly from this form, or you may make a further conversion to the more traditional outline form, or linear plan.

The linear plans below are formal outlines with Roman numerals, capital letters, and Arabic numbers. They preserve the main divisions (introduction, body, ending, appendix) and give them substantive labels: for example, the body in the first example is called "Description of benefits" in the linear plan. The body in the second example is divided in the linear plan into three separate sections: schedule of benefits and costs, length-of-service limitations, employee contributions. Under these divisions are grouped the principal assertions or facts that appear as random jottings within the respective sections of the nonlinear plan. Evidence and clarifications are subordinated under the main headings. It is of course possible—and often desirable, depending on the length and relative complexity of the material—to elaborate the divisions even further. Common sense dictates the specific form and the amount of elaboration of the outline.

TWO LINEAR OUTLINES   In the following outline, the material on the benefits package is arranged linearly for a brochure for new employees.

Control statement: Smurf, Inc. offers its employees an excellent benefits package that is carefully designed to provide needed protection and to extend compensation in tax-shielded ways.

I. Introduction
  A. Statement of company's commitment to provide excellent benefits
  B. Overview of comprehensive package
     1. Traditional
        a. Health
        b. Dental
        c. Life
        d. Disability
        e. FICA & company retirement plan
        f. Vacation & holidays
     2. Special
        a. Stock purchase
        b. Management club
        c. College tuition & books
  C. Plan is designed to
     1. Help meet emergencies, provide needed coverage, etc.
     2. Supplement direct compensation with benefits that have tax advantage to employees

II. Description of benefits
  A. Traditional
     1. Health (choice of Blue Cross/Blue Shield or HMO; employee contributions toward family coverage
     2. Dental
     3. Life (2 times salary)
     4. Long-term disability
     5. Retirement
        a. FICA
        b. Company plan (note eligibility requirements)
     6. Vacations & holidays

    B. Special
       1. Stock purchase (company match)
       2. Tuition & books for approved college courses
       3. Management club
III. Conclusion: reiteration of Smurf's goal of meeting employee needs through comprehensive package of benefits that are constantly reviewed and updated
IV. Appendix: full descriptions of each benefit, including costs, eligibility, etc.

In the next outline, the same information is tailored, again linearly, for a report from the Human Resources Development Department of Smurf, Inc. to the firm's president.

Control statement: Smurf, Inc. offers a competitive benefits package designed to maintain morale, reduce turnover, reward longevity, and control costs.

    I. Introduction
      A. Our benefits package is
        1. Competitive with other firms in our business and geographic area
        2. Important in maintaining employee morale and productivity and reducing turnover, which had previously been a special problem
        3. Carefully controlled to avoid abuse (note length-of-service limitations on many benefits)
        4. Cost effective (less than one-third of total salaries, which is well below average for a firm our size)
      B. Rest of report provides brief summary, concentrating on costs; full details are in Appendix
   II. Schedule of benefits and costs
      A. Total cost to firm is $7,917,708
      B. Average cost/employee is $6,522
      C. Benefits represent 32.6 percent of direct salaries
III. Length-of-service limitations help prevent abuse
      A. Dental (6 mos.)
      B. Disability (6 mos.)

   C. Stock purchase match (1 yr.)
   D. Tuition & books for approved courses (1 yr.)
   E. Co. retirement plan (1 yr.)
   F. Vacations (varies, rewards service)
IV. Employee contributions reduce burden to company
   A. Health (family contributions)
   B. Stock purchase
   C. Dental (increasing company participation to reward service)
   D. Tuition & books
   E. Company retirement (match)
 V. Conclusion: good package; Human Resources Development Department always ready to improve plan while meeting company goals, etc.
VI. Appendix: short table of costs

The linear plans shown above take the form of the outline typically taught in writing classes. This form is not, of course, the only correct kind of linear plan. The numbers and letters can be dropped; underlinings and typographical differentiation can be used; arrows and shapes can be employed. The specific form is certainly far less important than the underlying purpose: to convert nonlinear thinking into the framework of a document that must be read (if not necessarily written) linearly.

Checks on the Plan

Like the document based on it, the plan may be either for the record or for the reader. Some notes on the back of an envelope may serve you well. Or you may use a formal outline to coordinate other writers, set priorities, and obtain preliminary approvals. However you arrive at the plan, test the design before beginning to write the first sentence of the draft.

1. Is there one main idea, clearly indicated?
2. Does this idea meet the requirements of the assignment?
3. Are subpoints overtly tied to the main idea?
4. Is the relationship of subpoints to the main idea clear: do they illustrate, prove, contradict, clarify, add perspective?
5. Is the sequencing of information appropriate? What would happen if sections were reversed?
6. Are transitions between sections clear to build coherence?
7. Are any sections unintentionally contradictory? Any inconsistencies?
8. Have you justified the inclusion of all information?
9. Can anything be left out?
10. Are more (or fewer) examples needed to explain?
11. Is emphasis consistent?
12. Have you anticipated the reader's questions?
13. Have you isolated all possible information that can be presented visually?
14. Are headings functional? The headings in the outline move into the text to ease the reader's access to information. The outline becomes the table of contents, a tool many readers use to determine the document's pertinence. Where possible, prefer substantive terms to merely descriptive ones (prefer "Three Advantages of the Converter" to "Discussion"). Avoid an excess of levels of subheadings; two or three are usually enough.

A Writing Map

Planning writing is like mapping a route for a trip. Let's say you want to get from Chicago to Louisville by car in one day. You have established a purpose (to get to Louisville), a priority (by car), and a boundary condition (in one day). You look at the options in highways, then plot a course.

But suppose that as you locate the appropriate routes that will get you to Louisville in a day you discover on the map of

Indiana a small town noted for its architecture. You feel you *must* stop and see it, even though that means you will have to spend a night on the road. The stop represents a change in your original goal. The same detour can occur in planning a document. As you work through the map of the report or memo you are writing you may find yourself modifying your control statement, shifting subtly—or even boldly—the purpose of the piece. Similarly, as you begin driving to Louisville, you may remember a relative who lives in Indianapolis. If you stop to look him up, you must sacrifice the goal of arriving in Louisville that day. So again you make a shift, changing the route as you proceed.

Many people change plans as they write, too. The plan they carefully devised requires a modification that didn't become apparent until they put pen to paper. Making a plan may cause you to change the control statement because you are forced to rethink the context; writing the document may cause you to change the design that you created in the planning stages. As the turning point between analysis of the subject (context stage) and writing the document (product stage), planning is a gray area and is not subject to tight limits on time and function. This does not mean, however, that you can drift into the document without planning. It means that you have to regard planning as a dynamic function moving you from your assessment of the communications problem to the document that will solve the problem.

PRODUCT

From Design to Document

IN PLANNING, you sorted through your material to prepare it for transfer and designed the structure best able to carry it. That done, you're now ready to turn your plan into a document. You're ready to put words on paper (or on a computer terminal, if you're so inclined).

Starting

The plan should nudge you easily into writing. But even for professional writers, sometimes the worst part of writing is just getting started. Here are some suggestions for overcoming "writer's block," what one scientist calls "thesis paresis":

1. Warm up to writing on a major project by writing something small. Starting on a memo or letter helps get you in shape for the longer haul.
2. Begin to write at a point in the report you know well. You don't have to start at the introduction. Indeed, that's often best written last. Do the easy stuff first.

3. Limit the time you spend on writing (say, perhaps, two to three hours), concentrate, then take a break. Reward yourself when you've finished.

4. Or, set a page quota and quit when you've reached it.

5. Quit writing only when you know what your next section is going to be. Then when you return to writing—and have to start again—you'll know where to pick up.

6. Change your environment. One person's impossible prose was directly attributable to the location of his desk next to a drinking fountain. When he left his desk and wrote in the library, his prose vastly improved. Try writing someplace where you can avoid distractions.

7. Change your tools. If you're used to typing drafts, try longhand. Try different colored pens or pads. Try dictation. These seem like minor changes, but they may jolt your system into action.

8. If other techniques fail, try some variant of the way journalists often approach writing. They get the juices flowing by saying, "This is a story about. . . . " Then they fill in the blank. Try writing, "This is a report about. . . . " Or: "The purpose of this report is to. . . . " Or: "I am writing to. . . . " Then fill in the blank.

However you cajole yourself into starting, once you *have* started, keep going. Write as rapidly as you can, looking back only briefly to make sure you're on the track. Keep moving along your plan. After all, your writing consists merely in providing the connections among the points you have already established. Don't edit yet. Save that task for later, after your prose has cooled a bit.

Writing Paragraphs

As you write along your plan, think in terms of *division* and *connection*. Divide evidence into groups, each with one main point, one central core. Each grouping becomes a paragraph. This core may be dictated by the material—one month's work, one component of several, one step in a process, one factor in an analysis. Or it may be dictated by the reader. The core may match the reader's ability to focus attention and assimilate information. Thinking of paragraphing in terms of the reader means, for example, that easy material is effectively expressed in long paragraphs, difficult material in short. Paragraphing lets the reader know when the writer is shifting emphasis or entering a new topic. It eases skimming and rapid reading.

INTERNAL CONNECTIONS

Within paragraphs, evidence needs to be connected. The patterns for connections in general are those appropriate to the overall document: natural, logical, and psychological. Examples of paragraphs in each order are given on pages 33–34. The options for logical order are particularly rich. These include

- cause/effect
- general to particular (or particular to general)
- elimination of alternatives
- parallelism
- comparison/contrast
- classification

While you're writing, try for an engaging first sentence for each paragraph. That sentence sets up the content and form to follow and builds momentum for you as writer and for the reader. It predicts coherence and proper emphasis in the material that follows. Some writers fear making paragraph order too obvious. But most persons reading to be informed appreciate a form that eases access to material. Such forms may emerge only as you revise. Here's the draft of a paragraph:

Buses in the suburbs are not affected by the transit workers strike and should run according to regular schedules. Suburban trains into the city will run but may be more crowded than usual;

expect delays. The subway will not run. Buses will not run in the city. Trolley and bus lines which serve the suburbs will run. City trolleys will not run.

This paragraph has a core of evidence: effects of the strike on mass transportation. But it cries out for some classification and parallelism of expression. One revision divides the information into city and suburbs and conveys it in two parallel sentences:

In the city, no subways, trolleys, or buses will operate during the strike. In the suburbs, all buses, trolleys, and commuter trains will run, but expect crowding and delays.

Another division emphasizes what is and is not in operation:

All trains, buses, and trolleys operating outside and into the city are not affected by the strike and will operate, although crowding and delays are expected. No buses, trolleys, or subway lines will operate within the city.

Of course, you may also decide to classify the information into a table:

Not operating	*Operating*
City buses	Suburban buses
City trolleys	Suburban trolleys
Subway lines	Commuter trains

Write in the simplest form consistent with the material—and be aware of any opportunities to shift information into a visual (like the informal table above) that may have eluded you in the planning stage.

Here is another paragraph tracing a cause-effect (logical) relationship. The first sentence gives the total effect. The paragraph then details, in chronological order, the sequence of actions causing the effect. The end point of one action becomes the start of the next. The sentences are tied together through repetition (shown in italics). A major word in the predicate of one sentence becomes part of the subject of the next sentence (as shown in italics). This pattern is shown graphically in figure 4.1.

The formation of ice layers underneath the pavement causes frost heave. Although the temperature deep in the ground remains constant throughout the year, the temperature in the ground near the *surface* under the *pavement* fluctuates with air temperature. When the *pavement surface* freezes, the temperature in the ground under the pavement falls below *freezing*. The *freezing* and low temperatures induce *capillary tension* which sucks up water from the water table below. *This capillary tension* greatly increases the amount of *water* in the first zone under the pavement. When this *water* freezes, the soil expands far more than it otherwise would, and causes the pavement to heave.

As another example, here is an introductory paragraph. It begins with a generalization to encourage the reader (psychological order), then sets up steps in the process. The reader can expect the whole report is comprised of detailed discussions of each of these steps. The term "five" anticipates the five numbered items that follow. The structure of paragraphing in the whole report is shown graphically in figure 4.2.

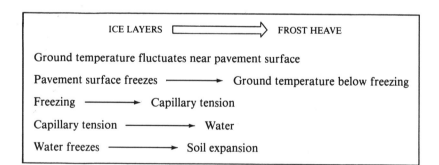

Figure 4.1
Graphic representation of paragraph on frost heave

The design of a sanitary sewer pumping station can be accomplished quickly and profitably if the engineer understands the design procedure. There are five basic steps in the design process:

1) Select the type of station, i.e., submersible, wetwell-drywell, wetwell-mounted drywell.
2) Establish the design flow
3) Calculate the total dynamic head
4) Select a pump and impeller
5) Size the wetwell[1]

Here is a paragraph from within a report that classifies evidence under a generalization:

Surprisingly, there appears to be an inverse relationship between distance from work to home and willingness to use mass transit. Willingness to use public transit decreases as distance between home and work increases. Sixty-three percent of the people responding to the PATS survey who lived within 5 miles of their place of work expressed "strong" or "very strong" willingness to use mass transit for daily commutation. This figure dropped to 52 percent for those living 6 to 10 miles from their work, and to 47 percent for those living 11 to 15 miles away. Only 29 percent of those living more than 15 miles from their place of work indicated "strong" or "very strong" willingness to use public transit daily. Even more significant is that nearly one half (49 percent) of the respondents in this group said they were "reluctant" to use mass transit. Differences in sex and age do not change the basic patterns of response.

These paragraphs are well connected. Each has a core of evidence. Each maintains a consistent point of view. Sentences lead into one another. In part, the sentence form makes those connections—a technique discussed later in this chapter. The paragraphs also provide overt directions to the reader about how to read. The "surprisingly" at the beginning of the last paragraph alerts the reader to an unex-

---

1. Reprinted by permission of Edmond C. Speitel.

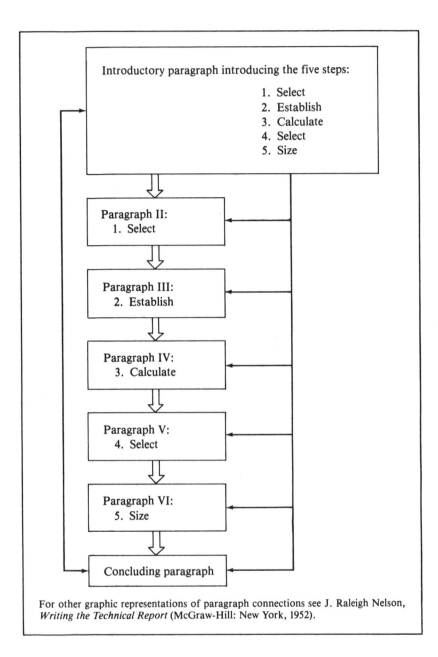

Figure 4.2
Graphic representation of paragraph sequence for a report on pumping
station design

pected result. Such words and phrases as *however, on the other hand, even more significant,* and *by contrast* provide further signs. Parallelism in form also underlines similarity in content and eases reading. Certain phrases—like "five basic steps"—presuppose other words.

EXTERNAL CONNECTIONS

Each paragraph, then, develops a core of evidence separate from other cores. But the paragraphs also have to work together to build a whole document. In effect, the first sentence, besides introducing the paragraph, bridges it to the paragraph before. Here's the paragraph that followed the one beginning "Surprisingly."

Variations in one factor, however, do affect the responses; among all three groups, the willingness to use public transit decreases as mean family income increases. Only 30 percent of those with incomes in excess of $45,000 express "strong" or "very strong" willingness to commute on public transportation, regardless of distance from work to residence. In fact, the variable of income is the best predictor of willingness to use mass transit. The relationship of this to the data on place of residence is clear: people with high incomes tend to live farther away from their place of work. Hence, the inverse relationship between distance between work and residence and willingness to use public transportation is merely a reflection of differences in income, with those having the highest income exhibiting the least desire to commute on mass transit.

The connection centers on substance: the issue of demographic factors. Structurally, the transition turns on a contrast word, *however,* and the link between "differences in sex and age" in the last sentence of the first paragraph with "one factor" in this paragraph. You should provide clear directional signals to the reader when you are getting started, changing topics, moving to another level of abstraction, introducing contrary evidence, drawing a major conclusion, citing illustrations, or ending. Look for opportunities to insert such transitional devices in revision. Moreover, in a long discussion, take time out to show the reader where you have been and where you are going, as in the following transitional paragraph:

Having looked now at the four major forces of change in today's savings and loan institutions—technology, inflation, consumerism, and competition—let us turn to some projections about the role of S&Ls in tomorrow's economy.

This paragraph adds no new information but assists the reader in remembering what has gone before and understanding what will come.

The paragraph, then, is a unit of the macrostructure of your document. Paragraphs are connected externally to achieve coherence in the whole. Such external connections may be a function of the control statement that ties everything together, or of subassertions that govern four or five paragraphs. The transitional paragraph above was preceded by four paragraphs, each about one force of change (in the order listed), and those paragraphs were preceded by an introduction naming the forces. Make the connections obvious.

Writing Sentences

Paragraphs divide and connect evidence in the macrostructure of writing. Sentences divide and connect evidence in the microstructure. Information can take different shapes within sentences to reflect your assessment of its importance, the impact you anticipate on the reader, and appropriate connections to other sentences in the paragraph. Examine, for example, the following propositions:

1. Ice forms in layers.
2. Ice forms underneath pavement.
3. Pavement can heave.

4. Heaves formed by ice are called *frost heaves*.
5. Ice underneath the pavement causes heaves.

These can be combined into one sentence:

6. The formation of ice layers underneath the pavement causes frost heaves.

Another example:

a. Dwellings must be designed.
b. Dwellings may be heated by the sun.
c. Dwellings heated by the sun are called *solar dwellings*.
d. Climate affects the design of solar heating systems.
e. Dwellings exist on a site.
f. The topography of the site affects the design of solar heating systems.

These can be combined into:

g. The design of a solar dwelling must be adapted to the climate and the topography of its site.

Propositions 1–5 and a–f can be called the *deep structure* of sentences 6 and g. Each sentence represents a different idea that is then tucked away in the final form of sentences 6 and g. The pattern of linkages in 6 and g is the *surface structure*. You need to adjust surface structure to match the plan of the paragraph, your ambitions for your material, and the reader's level of understanding. Tucking away an assumption may misdirect the reader. You may need to bring it into a sentence of its own. The process resembles somewhat the way equations are assembled. Sentence g, a balanced sentence in which the predicate imposes a condition on the subject, is particularly mathematical in organization. Like equations, sentences are governed by certain rules of operation. Here are some important ones:

1. Keep the main ideas accessible.
2. Express like ideas in parallel form.
3. Guard the verb.
4. Accept no false subjects.
5. Closely watch qualifiers.
6. Use punctuation effectively to divide and connect.
7. Control sentence length.

Let's look at each in detail.

1. KEEP MAIN IDEAS ACCESSIBLE

Depending on what you wish to emphasize, you might combine sentences 1–5 differently. For example:

• When ice forms in layers under pavement, frost heaves result.
• Frost heaves are caused by the formation of ice layers underneath pavement.
• Ice, which forms in layers under pavement, causes frost heaves.

Each surface structure provides a different setting for the material and a different impact on the reader. Within the bounds of some grammatical limits, choose the appropriate form. Sometimes you may wish to state a series of ideas separately in simple sentences, each bearing one concept, each a main clause, to give special emphasis to material and to build momentum for the reader. Or you may combine propositions by subordinating some to others. In subordinating, however, be careful. Embedded modifiers in the following sentence tear apart the subject and the verb, which should stand next to one another:

subject

A Teroidal *transformer* with heat removal in the form of a cylindrical ring, which is contiguous to the outside cylindrical surface of the core and which has edges, eliminated outside and located radially and evenly along the circle, when each of the edges is fixed in the central slot of the corresponding group of

edge radiators, forming a circular holder, with which the transformer is equipped, *is described* in this article.
                                     verb

Sometimes authors arrange sentence elements to build
anticipation rather than completing the main idea early as in
most English sentences. If you try this form, make sure you
do deliver in the end. Otherwise, you may, unlike the little
engine that could, come out with a sentence that couldn't,
like this one:

As projects become larger and more complex, as building technology changes, as costs rise dramatically and unpredictably, as
the "time is money" truism begins to pinch, as shortages and
uncertainties in the marketplace demand more responsive planning, as the amount of litigation grows and as the general level of
difficulty involved in accomplishing even simple projects seems
to increase at an alarming rate, almost all owners—private and
public—are taking pause before moving ahead too rapidly.

The sentence builds, but "taking pause before moving
ahead" is a vague, washed out climax. In general when the
thought is complex, keep the surface structure simple.
Sometimes, in an honorable but misguided attempt at conciseness (itself, of course, a desirable objective) writers
pack so much into a sentence that the reader can't find the
way through the maze. Keep main ideas accessible.

2. EXPRESS LIKE IDEAS IN PARALLEL FORM

Parallelism, as has been seen, works at the level of sections
of a document, in paragraphs, sentences, and even single
words (as in a series of headings). It creates a balance that
underscores the logic of your ideas and pleases the reader's
eye and ear. Properly used, parallelism becomes an art.
One author writes about a meeting of Congressional dele-
gates in this way:

It is a breakfast meeting with the usual fare: orange juice,
Danish pastry, coffee, accusations, and recriminations.

One technical editor said that parallelism problems account for 60 percent of the difficulties in the prose she edits. The concept of parallelism has two implications. First, the elements in a list must be logically equivalent. The logic of the list is indicated in an enumerator term, either expressed or understood. Second, the elements must be grammatically equivalent, that is, expressed in the same form. This form is established in the first term, which all others must follow. Knowing that each of the items in this form is equally weighted, the reader can read rapidly. He or she doesn't have to adapt to a change in pattern to receive information. Let's look at the concept in action:

Medical services that are not available from the college clinic include x-rays, cuts and lacerations requiring sutures, broken bones, and any ailment requiring hospitalization and surgery.

Clearly, this sentence is listing "services." The term "services" is the logical enumerator. Every item that follows in the list must be a service. "X-rays" is the first. This is a service, expressed as a noun. Other services, expressed as nouns, should follow. Instead, however, the list shifts, without telling the reader, to injuries rather than services. With luck, you don't get your cuts and lacerations at the clinic. The other items, too, are nouns, but they do not follow the logic of the enumerator. The sentence breaks down.
Here's another problem in a faulty enumerator:

Health officials should be concerned, whether it's smoking, asthma, air pollution, or any other lung illness.

"Other lung illness" means that each of the items can be classified as such an illness; but smoking and air pollution are possible causes, not illnesses. Yet another example:

Essential elements of technology transfer include: patent literature, published literature, exchange of personnel, licensing agreements, self-help programs, joint ventures involving several countries, selling high technology hardware, and building facilities for manufacturing in the country.

The sentence runs awry in part because the enumerator term "elements" is too vague. It allows for too much over-lapping in the items. One could sell high technology through a licensing agreement. A self-help program might be a joint venture. Whenever possible, avoid "things," "factors," and "elements" as enumerators. Your logic will be cleaner if you can limit the list from the start. (The last two items in this list, by the way, are also not grammatically parallel.)

Logic further breaks down when the items in the list have dissimilar charges, that is, some are expressed as neutral quantities, some as positive or negative. The charges should match.

Constraints are imposed on an engineer's activities by such factors as space, time, energy, and incomplete information.

The first three items are expressed as neutrals, although the enumerator "constraints" signals a list of negatives, as in "incomplete information."

One recasting:

An engineer's activities are constrained by the limits of space, time, energy, and information.

In addition to being logically parallel, lists must be gram-matically parallel as well. That is, each item should be expressed in the same form as the first item.

He needed time to plan, to design, and for contacting the customer.

That last item wiggled out of the form. It should be recast: "to contact the customer."

3. GUARD THE VERB

As the verb goes, so goes the sentence. Much of the writing of professionals implies action. But you'd never know that if you simply made a list of the verbs (which should carry the action) in professional reports. The list centers on "is," "are," "do," "get," "make," "involves," "use"—verbs to be sure, but dilute forms. The real action is smothered someplace in the sentence. The reader has to hunt for it. Instead, pull the verb out of the noun or adjective form shading it and let it shine. The reward is greater efficiency and emphasis in the sentence, improved clarity and conciseness, and a shorter reading time, something a reader always appreciates.

Dilute: The forging of the blade was done properly.
Strong: The blade was properly forged.

Dilute: Mating of grizzlies takes place in May.
Strong: Grizzlies mate in May.

Dilute: An analysis was made of the test data.
Strong: We analyzed the test data.

Dilute: For purposes of summarization a listing of these factors is included below.
Strong: To summarize, these factors are listed below.

Most of the action in the following paragraph stagnates in the nouns. The author meant to emphasize problems in the process. Stronger verbs would help, as in the revised version.

ORIGINAL

Systems engineering participation in the design of computer programs for the X project stops with the generation of the functional requirements. Software design teams take these requirements and begin the program design process with little interaction with systems engineering. Misinterpretation of requirements, which is unavoidable on any large program, is not detected until the program test when the design is complete. At this stage program changes are costly.

RECAST

In the design of computer programs for the X project, systems engineering draws up the functional requirements. Software design teams then design the program based on these requirements. These teams, however, interact only rarely with systems engineering during the design. If they misinterpret any requirements, an unavoidable situation on any large program, they do not detect the error until the program test when the design is complete. At this stage program changes are costly.

Sometimes, of course, you might want to emphasize the names of the action. The language allows you to do this. Go ahead. But often you tie down the meaning better if you cast the action in strong verbs.

Guarding the verb also means not overusing the passive voice. You need to use the passive when there simply is no actor to assign responsibility to:

During the fire, several noxious gases were produced.

But sometimes the passive appears even when there is a clear and present actor. It seems to sound objective or impersonal. The reader has told you she objects to "I" or "we" in a report. Constraints against naming the researcher may be loosening, however. The passive conflicts with a goal of conciseness since, by definition, passives trail helping verbs and often prepositional phrases. Passives also tolerate vagueness:

The meeting was set for 10 A.M.

Who set the time? The sentence doesn't say. Passives are sometimes necessary, but for clarity and conciseness, keep active.

In guarding the verb, observe, too, certain conventions of tense use.

- What an individual *did* is presented in the past tense.

    In the evaluation, we *examined* 14 specimens.
- The implications of the action are presented in the present tense.

    On the basis of these evaluations we *conclude* that the agent *is* indeed toxic and *produces* deleterious effects upon specimen cells.
- Interpretations held to be currently valid are presented in the present tense.

    Jones and McKim (1974) *describe* a technique similar to that used in our experiments.
- General descriptions of a process are usually given in the present tense.

    When fluoride is introduced into the system, the result is better dental health. (Not, by the way, "will be.")
- The past progressive tense is used only for an action begun in the past and continued into the present.

    Wrong: I *have presented* the results in 1978.
    Right: I *presented* the results in 1978. (The act belongs in the past tense as an act now completed.)
    Right: I *have been* working on the project since January.

4. ACCEPT NO FALSE SUBJECTS

Writers probably have more problems with verbs, the action words, than with nouns, the namers. You often know what you want to talk about, but you don't know how to predicate it, how to tie down the actor to action. Sometimes, however, even the topic is blurred, or you change the topic in the middle of a sentence, seduced by a more interesting noun. Tell the reader about the substitution. Here are some unruly sentences:

The need for more effective fertilizers is required.

The real subject here is *fertilizers*. They are required (or needed).

The source materials with which all education must begin is research.

The author intended *source* as the subject, but *materials* broke in. The verb agrees with source—a singular noun.

Lawyers for 13 persons convicted of marijuana smuggling and conspiracy charges last Wednesday in federal court were given 20 days to file post-trial motions or face up to 10 years in prison and $30,000 in fine.

"Why hasn't someone thought of this before?" comments *The New Yorker* on this item from the *Key West Citizen*.

A subset of the rule on false subjects governs the use of pronouns. They are often abused, as the following example shows.

Do not dump the garbage in the gutter. *It* is not sanitary.

What's unsanitary—garbage, gutter, dumping?

Eight companies are having problems with their income tax reports. *These* are being investigated.

The companies or the reports?

So if my taxes are paying people to smell diesel engines, you might ask how come *they* still smell?

Who smells?

Let the reader know what the pronoun stands for. Use pronouns to foster continuity:

Control systems play a key role in management in the large corporation. *They* allow top managers to monitor divisional preference. *They* prevent waste and fraud. Control systems also aid management in allocating resources within the firm.

Readers can also become annoyed when writers move the subjects of sentences around unnecessarily. Often, an easy recasting of the sentence can maintain subject consistency and ease the reader's lot, as in this example:

The module was removed from the chamber and visual inspection performed.

The sentence is more efficient if the subject is kept the same:

The module was removed from the chamber and visually inspected.

The subject in the following sentence is too dense. It's unclear who the actors are. A recasting shows the real nature of the subject.

ORIGINAL

Customer schedule concern expressed at the system architecture and functional requirements review caused me to reevaluate our system design.

RECAST

At the review of the system architecture and functional requirements, the customers expressed concern about the schedule. Their concern caused me to reevaluate our system design.

5. CLOSELY WATCH QUALIFIERS

Between and around the subject and the verb comes the rest of the sentence. You can modify, set conditions, subordinate. But unless you watch qualifiers, they can take over a sentence. Modifiers can snuff out good intentions and run off with emphases of their own. You can vary the extent and position of qualifiers to achieve emphasis and continuity with other sentences. But check that the qualifier is on the right element:

The heat is mostly carried upwards.

Heat will go up. What the author intended was that *most of the heat* escaped from the system.

The qualifying element should also sit next to the item it qualifies in the sentence and should not dangle. A modifier dangles when it has nothing to modify or cannot logically modify the noun or pronoun it is hanging around. To correct: supply the right subject.

ORIGINAL

Lacking enough time to edit, the memo was longer than I had intended.

The memo is not capable of lacking time. Only a person can do this.

CORRECTED

Lacking enough time to edit, I wrote a longer memo than I had intended.

OR

Because I lacked enough time to edit, the memo was longer than I had intended.

6. USE PUNCTUATION EFFECTIVELY TO DIVIDE AND CONNECT

Punctuation is an important tool for showing readers what words should be read together and what words are part of another set. Punctuation also builds anticipation (the role of the colon), joins clauses to avoid a fragmentation of sentences (one role of the semicolon), and sorts out modifiers before a noun (the role of the hyphen). Punctuation alone can't overcome a poorly constructed sentence, but as a good signalling device it can encourage understanding. Here are some guidelines:

1. Use the comma (,) to

• separate independent clauses in a compound sentence with a coordinating conjunction:
  The building lacked adequate storage and an adequate heating system(,) but we loved it anyway for its style.
• separate elements in a list:
  He brought to his job determination(,) good technical understanding(,) and hope.
• set off a long dependent clause or phrase at the beginning of a sentence:
  Because there was not enough time to assess its true worth(,) we had to guess.
• set off a nonrestrictive clause or phrase:
  The solution(,) which was supplied by the X company(,) was ineffective.

In this last sentence, the clause in commas merely adds information about the noun but doesn't restrict the noun. If the clause is meant to limit the noun, then no commas are used. Another meaning attaches to the following sentence from that of the one above:

The solution that was supplied by the X company was ineffective.

This statement makes an implied comparison with other, effective solutions. Note, too, that in traditional usage "which" is nonrestrictive and "that" is restrictive.

2. Use the semicolon (;) to

• separate independent clauses in a compound sentence without a conjunction:
  The comptroller's office was enraged(;) the president's office was thrilled.

· separate elements in a list when the elements are lengthy or contain other punctuation:

> The conditions included wide political participation, which was expected(;) low incomes, which were not(;) and party loyalty.

3. Use the colon (:) to

· build anticipation. Use before examples, equations, explanations, illustrations, and in some conventional ways, such as in expressions of time, volume, and the like.

> He told his people they needed to know only one principle(:) Watch the bottom line.
>
> This process is summarized in the following equation(:)

$$x = \sum_{y=7} \frac{a - bk}{y}$$

> The combination of finite element analysis and experimental models is also a strong approach to addressing the question(:) Can an optimized plate be designed?

7. CONTROL SENTENCE LENGTH

Short sentences are usually easier to read than long sentences. This concept is the underlying assumption of most tests of readability. Of course, too many short sentences in a row may fail to show proper linkage. The reader may feel reduced to the days of primers about happy animals in the forest. Too many long sentences in a row, however, risk a worse fate: the reader may get lost, be forced to reread, not comprehend. As a general rule, keep sentences under twenty words. Whenever you have three long sentences tied together, make the next one short. When you sit down to write, you won't have before you a plan of sentence lengths: sentence 1 = 20 words; sentence 2 = 15 words. But when you *re*write, then count.

Final Inspection

*Re*writing is usually part of the process of writing. But editing—whether of your own or of someone else's work—is too often approached with eyes peeled to note any error, especially small ones, and red pencil at the ready. Editing is better thought of as the task of managing writing, pulling together in a final inspection at the end all the pieces that had to be created to reach the purpose and priorities you set. Routines for doing this vary. Some suggestions follow for editing your own and reviewing someone else's prose. But whatever the routine, the key is to revise in stages. Each stage in checking should focus on one particular phase in the writing process, as the rest of this chapter shows.

EDITING YOUR OWN WRITING

Some authors rewrite a draft as they go along, returning at the end of a page or section to straighten up their words. Other writers, especially reluctant ones, are better off to simply finish a draft, then go back after they've gained perspective to look for improvements. Any revision routine is highly personal, but here are some suggestions:

1.   Read your prose aloud to hear how it sounds.
2.   Make a list of the headings in your draft—an outline from the draft. Match it against your original plan and your intentions for the material. See if your direction is clear and the directional signals are consistent.
3.   Write or type the draft with enough room between the lines to note corrections.
4.   Spread out five or six pages—a section or a whole document—beside each other on a table to see how the discussion is advancing without the artificial segmentation of individual sheets of paper.
5.   Make a separate list of all figures and tables as you work through the draft and check for consistency in numbering.

6. Read through the draft once, making notes to yourself on what needs to be done—but not actually making any changes.

7. Cut and tape pieces of the draft to move sections around if necessary.

8. Ask a colleague to read the draft and offer suggestions.

9. When your draft becomes unreadable, as it may, with too many notes and changes, type up a new draft. Word processors, of course, make this step easy.

10. In a large project, develop a routine for disposing of drafts. With each draft you may make several copies for circulation and review. When you've received the comments, consolidate these on one master copy, which you keep perhaps in a three-ring notebook for ease of reference. Throw out the other copies. Otherwise, you may find yourself unable to tell which is the corrected version.

REVIEWING SOMEONE ELSE'S WRITING

In general, the approach to revision which you apply to your own writing should work as you review the writing of others. But a little additional advice may be in order:

1. Before someone or a group of people writes for you, make sure you set out the context for the assignment. Analyze the boundary conditions, options, priorities, and purpose. Circulate this analysis in a memo or perhaps an abstract or summary that coordinates the team. Settle any differences in perception about what the document should be and do. Assign specific tasks and deadlines. Then stick to the standard. Don't be arbitrary.

2. For long writing projects, schedule intermediate conferences to check that the document is shaping up as you both (or all) want. Look over an outline to see if the emphasis is appropriate and the evidence is adequate and properly sequenced.

3. In reviewing a draft, control the impulse to rewrite. Editing is repair work, not construction. The problems of writing new paragraphs or sections are that (1) you're liable

to misunderstand the writer's point and therefore change the substance of the passage; (2) you may introduce a new style or tone that clashes with the original.

4. Let the writer do his or her own rewriting. This will reinforce patterns of appropriate prose and ease your job with subsequent documents.

5. Be specific in criticism. Don't just turn the document back in a flourish of such generalizations as "I just don't like it" or "It's not what I wanted." Write a summary of your criticisms for a long report. Use consistent notations. (Base your evaluation on the checklists presented under "Levels of Editing.")

6. Don't nitpick. The writer only has so much energy for revision. Don't waste that energy by presenting too many minor criticisms. Focus your criticism on main points.

7. Remember to praise good work, to cite places where the writer handled material particularly well. Being appreciated helps one forge ahead. We all need praise.

LEVELS OF EDITING

As a managerial process editing has much in common with auditing; both are control functions intended to assure that the final product is and does what it is supposed to.

The analogy is worth extending. Three levels of auditing are commonly recognized: level I (financial, which is concerned with the actual entries, the details); level II (economic, which is concerned with efficiency); level III (program, which is concerned with effectiveness). By analogy we can see three levels of managerial editing:

I: word by word
II: efficiency
III: effectiveness

Such a three-phase check matches the outcome in a piece of writing against your intentions. Resist the temptation to begin at level I. Instead, begin at the highest level. Look at the project as a whole to determine the responsiveness of the final document to the context. You may need to rearrange whole sections to clarify the control statement. You may eliminate sections. Then, at level II, check the organization and the distribution of information to visual or verbal forms. Finally, at level I, check how the sentences are running, if the headings are parallel, and if you've used the right words and punctuation. Proofread for typos. Writers who begin the process at level I—and many do—often spend hours tediously marking up several pages only later to discover, at level III, that the sections aren't pertinent and should be scrapped. So save the close work for the end.

CHECKLIST FOR THREE-LEVEL EDITING

Level III Editing
To clarify the control statement (see also pp. 23–26):

1. Place main points up front.
2. Establish a framework for your presentation. Make the plan obvious.
3. Show the reader how the subject at hand affects him or her.
4. Distinguish the new from the well known.

Level II Editing
To make organization more effective (see also pp. 32–36):

1. Check the introduction. Does it drag, with too much background that delays the reader? Or does it try to tell everything at once and thus overwhelm the reader?
2. Analyze headings. Add headings where necessary. Check parallelism in logic and form. Check adherence to the conventions appropriate to your company and to the reader.
3. Make certain that every statement of every section bears on the subject as defined by the heading of that section.
4. Build in generalizations in advance of details to aid the reader in assimilating new information. Summarize periodically in a long report and forecast the next section.

5. Break up long paragraphs.
6. Look for opportunities for cross-referencing.

To balance verbal and visual expression:

1. Make sure all visuals are accounted for in the text.
2. Place data in a visual; use the text to explain.
3. Use captions on visuals to assist the reader in knowing what to look for.
4. Avoid excessive overlap between visuals and text.
5. Make sure text and visuals are consistent in information and interpretations.

Level I Editing

To streamline expression (see also pp. 64–75):

1. Be precise and as simple as possible in word choice, especially verbs. Don't merely reissue standard jargon.
2. Eliminate unnecessary words:

• redundancies like *future potential, fellow colleagues, collaborate together*
• flabby connective phrases like *due to the fact that* (for *because*), *for the purpose of* (to), *in the event of* (if)
• excessive expletives and other postponers, as in this sentence:

> It has often been said and it is likely to be believed by people throughout the private and public sectors of the community that good health is a prerequisite of good work.

3. Don't mix images. Here's one bad mixture: "Screw on your ingenuity cap in order to hit those bells and whistles that turn the evaluator's ticker ticking."
4. Use only those abbreviations known to the reader and standard for the field. When in doubt, give full information on the first mention.
5. Break up long sentences.
6. Express main ideas in main clauses and keep qualifiers in line.
7. Proofread for spelling and punctuation. For letter-perfect copy, try proofing backwards, the last word in the

document first, then the second-to-last, and so on. That avoids the trap of reading along in context. Or have someone read the text aloud as you check another copy.

The three levels of auditing and editing, of course, match the three stages in the writing process. Level III checks on the context. Level II checks on the plan. And level I checks on the product. Such a final inspection helps assure that your writing is effective and efficient.

Finishing

How do you know when to call the latest draft the final one? When do you know your polishing is complete? As a carpenter once said, you can sand forever. You can also keep tampering with a text, fine-tuning until even you aren't sure if the revision is better or worse than the original. Indeed, sometimes it isn't. Of ten drafts of the U.S. Constitution, for example, it was the second that was finally adopted. The deadline set for the assignment may force an end. Your own sense that you have solved the communications problem is also to be trusted if you defined the problem well and applied the checks for appropriateness.

One engineer in a large corporation defines a good report as one that "goes away." When he has checked it over and sent it on, he doesn't want to see it again. In a sense, his definition is valid. A report or proposal or article or brochure or letter is instrumental. It should go into the system and do its work. In addition, it represents your skills as a professional: your competence with your material, your attitude toward the reader, your understanding of the reader's needs. The written document is the point of confluence of many forces. It is the product of a process that begins with a problem and moves through many decisions to an appropriate solution.

· 5 ·

FORMS FOR
PROFESSIONAL
WRITING

WRITING IS A PROCESS for giving documentary shape to material under a series of constraints. The availability of information, the time to digest it, the needs of one or a number of readers, the purpose for which you want to deploy the information—all these, as this guide has shown, help shape a document. The most apparent shaper is the form in which the material is to be presented. Unlike reader expectation and communications purpose, form is visible—you can *see* that a memo is different from a letter. Forms are aids in patterning material.

Indeed, one of the marks of writing in the professions is the availability and importance of forms. Much writing fits into conventional patterns, and knowing these patterns eases the structuring of material into an effective document. You might collect models of good writing within typical forms as they cross your desk. This chapter, too, offers advice on several of the most popular forms of professional prose. Forms, of course, vary: a memo written for an agency of the government of California has a slightly different appearance from one written for IBM. Every company has its own sanctioned letter form. Articles submitted to *Scientific American* must conform to different rules from those that apply at the *Journal of Accountancy*. The rule is that you follow the form—the conventions—of the organization for which you work or the one to which you submit a document.

But within the variations certain general principles can be identified for each major form of professional writing. The advice here stresses those principles; as always in writing, you have to modify to fit prevailing standards.

Abstracts and Executive Summaries

Abstracts and executive summaries are forms of writing that summarize other documents. The term *abstract* is usually used for scientific and technical summaries in academic settings as well as professional journals and meetings. Abstracts vary in length, but most are no longer than 300 words. The term *executive summary* usually refers to the summary of a corporate or government report or proposal in a business setting. Summaries tend to be longer than abstracts—they may run 20–30 pages for a 300–1000 page document.

As the name implies, an abstract distills the central message of a document. Abstracts may be written in advance of the document; often abstracts of papers to be presented at meetings must be submitted to the program committee six months or more in advance as the basis of selection for presentation. Or you may write an abstract when you've finished writing the paper. Abstracts may be published with the parent document or collected separately, in a meeting program or in such reference tools as *Chemical Abstracts* that guide readers to the literature.

Definitions vary about what exactly constitutes an abstract, but in general two forms are recognized: the topical and the informative. The *topical abstract* is simply one or a few sentences listing the topics covered in the parent document but not revealing information or conclusions about the topics:

This paper looks at house pattern books published in nineteenth-century America with a particular focus on *The Architecture of Country Houses* by A. J. Downing (1850).

The *informative abstract* doesn't just talk about the paper but talks about the investigation itself and summarizes the chief conclusions (and recommendations, if appropriate):

In nineteenth-century America, a widely felt need for information on house building resulted in a sizable body of literature that addressed homes as both fact and symbol and developed a form and a language for conveying architectural information to a broad middle-class audience. One of the most popular of the house pattern books was A. J. Downing's *The Architecture of Country Houses* (1850). Downing was an effective popularizer of architectural information whose language dealt simply and effectively with both the technical details of building, plumbing, ventilation, and heating, and the cultural and symbolic aspects of home in a period of great change and growing concern for developing an American architecture.

In writing the abstract, focus on results and implications, not on the details of materials and methods, unless the method is indeed what is new. Avoid becoming bogged down:

A 72-gram brown Rhode Island Red country-fresh candled egg was secured and washed free of feathers, etc. Held between thumb and index finger, about 3 feet more or less from an electric fan (General Electric Model No. MC-2404 Serial Number JC 23023, nonoscillating, rotating on "high" speed at approximately 1052.23 ± 0.02 rpm), the egg was suspended on a string (pendulum) so it arrived at the fan with essentially zero velocity normal to the fan rotation plane. The product adhered strongly to the walls and ceiling and was difficult to recover; however, with the use of putty knives a total of 13 grams was obtained and put in a skillet with 11.2 grams of hickory smoked Armours old-style bacon and heated over a low Bunsen flame for 7 minutes and 32 seconds. What there was of it was excellent scrambled eggs.

This abstract drowns in details. Instead, focus on the main point:

Very good scrambling was produced by throwing an egg into an electric fan. The product was difficult to recover from the walls and ceiling, but the small amount that was recovered made an excellent omelet. A shrouded fan was designed to improve the yield, in preparation for additional experiments.[1]

GUIDELINES FOR WRITING

To write the abstract, work from your outline or table of contents, which should indicate chief topics and their sequencing. Many writers have found that creating an abstract before they settle into a whole document aids them in the final writing. They know how the story comes out. An abstract or executive summary also helps direct a team in a multiple-author project. Keep these suggestions in mind:

1. Include the control statement from the parent document.
2. Include the most important second-level assertions.
3. Omit minor details.
4. Make sure the abstract is readable without reference to the parent document.
5. Use complete sentences.
6. Eliminate any redundancy and weak connectors; reduce paragraphs in the original to sentences, sentences to phrases, phrases to single words.
7. Conform to the style of the journal or organization in matters of usage of mathematical notations and visuals.

To write the executive summary, follow this same advice, but you can allow yourself more room for details and visuals.

---

1. *The D(ratted) P(rogress) R(eport)*, July 1954. Published by the Savannah River Plant of the Department of Energy, Aiken, So. Carolina. Reprinted with permission.

The name indicates that readers are executives, which is partly true in that the summary often features the management aspects of the parent document. But that distinction doesn't always hold. Essentially everyone who is likely to read any section of the parent document will read the summary to find a framework for understanding the technical discussion that follows. The executive summary that accompanies a proposal is often a glossy sales document, with pictures and statistics that highlight the proposer's good idea and effective track record. The summary justifies why the company should be chosen to do the work. Summaries of reports, too, often provide the proof as well as the generalizations. The summary is a major business tool. In these days of inflation in prose (as in other segments of life), the executive summary serves as a quick read into the information, which may be conveyed in other sections for the record, but hardly read. Give enough information for the reader to make a decision.

Memos

Memos are written up, down, and sideways on the corporate organizational chart. Lots of people complain about "memo mania," the excess of paper floating from desk to desk. The mania is not likely to stop, but you can make your memos effective if you keep a few thoughts in mind in writing them.

GUIDELINES FOR WRITING

1. Write one memo on one topic. Focus the memo on one self-contained and fairly simple unit of information: date of the next bloodmobile visit, new procedure for feeding laboratory animals, report on a trip, congratulations on a job well

done. If you have information from two different contexts to convey, even to the same reader, write two memos. They may need to go on separately to other readers or into separate files.

2. Keep the memo to one page. You may attach supporting documentation in the form of tables or figures, but try to keep the text to one page for maximum impact on the reader. All readers consider themselves too busy to read most memos. You have a better chance of being read if you don't tax them beyond one page.

3. Use a subject heading on the memo that indicates its content and your approach. Don't just head it, "Subject: Report," but, for example, "Subject: Recommendations for compliance with regional water-saving measures."

4. Date all memos. These documents become records and as such need to be located in time.

5. Prune distribution lists. Some people send copies of memos to just about everybody as a matter of course. Instead, gain a reputation for writing only to those people who need the information, and only when they absolutely need it. That reputation will increase your likelihood of being read.

6. Begin the memo with a sentence which answers this question in the reader's mind: "Why am I [the reader] reading this memo on this topic from you [the writer] now?"

7. Use short paragraphs, including lists and numbered steps where appropriate. Exploit the use of attachments for details.

8. Use headings to highlight and to increase reader accessibility to your information.

9. End with an action line if you are requesting some action from the reader.

A model memo is shown in figure 5.1. This memo circulated within an engineering firm. The author, a project engineer, deliberately avoids using "I" or other indicators of authorship. He writes in a corporate voice, emphasizing the need for the monthly progress reports, their form, and their advantages to both the customer and the investigators. The tone is didactic and formal. The instructions are concise and specific.

MEMO

Date: June 12, 1982

To: Principal Investigators on Contract NAS 532-80

From: C. Croney, Project Engineer   *C.C.*

Subject: Form for Monthly Progress Reports

1. Formal monthly progress reports are a requirement of Contract NAS 532–80. Since many different groups are working in support of this effort, a standard format for these reports is necessary. The format described in section 2 is to be used by each Principal Investigator.

2. FORMAT

   a. Header: task title and principal investigator's name

   b. Paragraph 1: Task objective—a brief description of the task's activities and relationship to the contract

   c. Paragraph 2: Work summary—a description of the work completed during the current month

   d. Paragraph 3: Accomplishments—a summary of all accomplishments since the contract start date

   e. Paragraph 4: Problems—a summary of problems encountered during the current month with proposed solutions

3. The report should be limited to two pages. References should be used to cite additional information when necessary. Each report should be typed and submitted to the project office three business days after the end of each month.

4. The customer will better understand our efforts if our reports are clear and concise. These reports should also assist each Principal Investigator in tracking and coordinating his or her group's efforts.

Courtesy of Charles Croney.

Figure 5.1
Model memo

Letters

Letters are much like memos, although they tend to adhere to more complex conventions of style and are often external documents where memos circulate within a company or agency. Letters are designed to match many different contexts. In fact, so many of these contexts are predictable that books of form letters sell well. To use these forms, you simply have to fill in the blanks. Instantly you then achieve, for example, a letter of complaint (or adjustment of the complaint if you are on the other side); a letter introducing a salesperson, or inviting business, or inviting or thanking a guest speaker, or acknowledging a kindness, or expressing a grief.

Writing from scratch, however, is not that difficult if you understand the needs of the information, purpose, and reader and adjust your approach accordingly. Moreover, your own version will have a clearer ring of authenticity than the canned one. Use whatever conventional style your company endorses or you prefer (the model in figure 5.3 shows the block form). Within that style (a clear boundary condition), check for the following.

GUIDELINES FOR WRITING

1. Think of the reader. Some people call this requirement of letters (and memos) the "you attitude." The letter should not just be a string of I's but an acknowledgment of the point of view of the reader—"you." In addressing someone in a letter, you are often beginning or continuing a relationship; watch the tone and maintain good will.

2. Get to the point. Within the need for courtesy, begin directly. Don't waste the reader's time with frivolous preliminaries.

3. Use short paragraphs and sentences.

4. Keep to one page (with attachments if necessary; see model).

5. Don't fall back on letterish cliches such as "I am in

Thank you very much for considering the implementation of a series of workshops on personnel practices. I have had many conversations with my colleagues as to the programming of the workshops. Although this proposed scheduling is tentative, we do not anticipate much variation particularly with regards to the workshop topics. The first workshop will be held here in Columbus and will focus on the theme of management for retention. It will probably take place sometime in June. The academic participants in that workshop will be myself, Dr. Andrew Rennick of Case-Western Reserve, Dr. Peter Morris of Ohio University, and Dr. Anne Christos of the University of Kentucky. The second workshop will on women as managers. It is scheduled to be held in the latter part of August, possibly in Chicago, Illinois. The reason for choosing Chicago as the site is that I would like to have Drs. David Kidd and Neil Bacon, both of whom are at the University of Chicago, attend. Moreover, this will give us the opportunity to attract corporate leaders and program managers from another industrial base. On September 8th and 9th the third workshop, which is on standards for promotion, will be held in Washington. A select group of managers from Fortune 500 companies will be in attendance. This workshop will include three academic leaders— Drs. Hagland, Kirby, and myself—and three people from industry. A fourth workshop on retirement preparation dealing with preretirement programs

Figure 5.2
Draft of text for model letter

and other programs for financial planning and counseling will be directed primarily at training directors. The fifth workshop will be directed toward innovative personnel programs in operation now in major corporations and an assessment of the responsibilities of corporations toward personnel practices. The scheduling and the individuals specifically to be involved in the last two workshops have not yet been finalized. In addition, a sixth workshop with the authors of the proceedings and key individuals who have been identified in the course of the previous workshops will be held here in Columbus to summarize the information for the proceedings. We anticipate that the text should be completed by the end of the summer (1984).

Each workshop will be limited to less than twelve participants. Professors Morris, Kirby, and I, as authors of the proceedings, will attend all sessions. The ultimate goal of these workshops will be to produce a coherent and practical guide on the current status of personnel practices. It is the intent of the authors to produce not only a scholarly basis for future examinations but, more importantly, a manual which will be of immediate assistance to corporate managers.

You will find enclosed an estimate of the costs of the workshops. Any suggestions or assistance you can render in this regard will be greatly appreciated. Thank you again for the opportunity to initiate this program and I am looking forward to a successful endeavor.

February 24, 1983

James T. Bennett
Senior Vice President
X Corporation
12 West Broad Street
Columbus, OH 43210

Dear Jim,

Thank you for considering the implementation of a series of workshops on
personnel practices.

The attached sheet lists proposed workshop topics, the names of expert
leaders and anticipated participants, and tentative dates and locations. As
you'll see, we still need to fill a few leader positions. We should have these
names by the beginning of April. Each workshop will be limited to about
twelve participants. The structure of the sessions reflects extensive discussions
with colleagues. We suggest that the third workshop be held in Chicago
because both Dr. Kidd and Dr. Bacon are at the University of Chicago and
because a session there should allow us to attract corporate leaders and
program managers from that area.

In addition to fostering discussion among participants, the workshops will
lead to a published proceedings which can serve as a manual on the subject.
It will be coauthored by Professor Peter Morris, Professor Donna Kirby, and
me. We will attend all workshops and will schedule a sixth session with key
individuals identified in the workshops to summarize information. We
anticipate completion of the proceedings by September 1984. The text
should be both a scholarly reference work and a manual of immediate assistance to corporate managers.

A tentative budget for the workshops is also enclosed. We will greatly appreciate your suggestions on this.

Again, thank you for the opportunity to develop this program. I am looking
forward to a successful endeavor.

Sincerely yours,

Brian Wier

Brian Wier
Associate Professor of Management Science

encs.

Figure 5.3
Revised model letter

WORKSHOPS ON PERSONNEL PRACTICES

Topic	Leaders	Expected participants	Date	Location
1. Management for retention	B. Wier (Ohio State); A. Rennick (Case Western Reserve); P. Morris (Ohio Univ.); A. Christos (Univ. of Ky.)	Personnel managers	June ——	Columbus
2. Women as managers	D. Kidd and N. Bacon (Univ. of Chicago); someone from industry	Broad representation from the Chicago area	August ——	Chicago
3. Standards for promotion	B. Hagland (MIT); D. Kirby (Ohio State); B. Wier (Ohio State); E. Drott (IBM); J. Lieberthal (ITT); T. Williard (Borden Inc.)	Managers from large corporations (Fortune 500)	Sept. 8, 9	Washington
4. Retirement preparation	Open	Training directors	Open	Columbus
5. Innovative programs/ assessment of corporate responsibilities	Open	Personnel managers	Open	Open

receipt of yours of the 19th"; or, "This letter is written pursuant to our telephone conversation."

Figure 5.2 presents a draft of the text for a model letter. Figure 5.3 shows the final revised model letter and one of its attachments.

Proposals

Proposals are the start of something new. They define a method of attack on a problem or present an answer to a question. Two kinds of proposals are commonly recognized: the solicited and the unsolicited. The solicited proposal is written in response to a *request for proposal* (RFP). The requester—a potential sponsor of research or a customer— poses the problem or question. An unsolicited proposal derives from your own initiative. You have, for example, an idea for speeding up the collection of receivables. You then suggest your idea to someone who can profit from it. As a general rule, a solicited proposal sells the answer while an unsolicited proposal sells the problem—and then the answer.

With lots of variation in the form, proposals are a staple of life in both the public and private sectors. You may have seen—or written—one that is one page long and others that are more aptly measured in meters than in pages. Some mystery surrounds proposal writing, in part because proposals have great financial value. The proposal brings in the grant or the contract. Proposal writing is often centered in the marketing division of a company, a reasonable assignment since a proposal is a marketing tool. It is a sales document and as such must be groomed to persuade the reader to buy. The process of reader analysis is particularly important in writing a proposal. Everything must be shaped to convince.

An RFP usually stipulates a form for the proposal— specific steps or sections that must be present. Follow it. If you aren't given a particular form, and especially if you are submitting an unsolicited proposal, then consider structuring your material in the sections indicated below.

SECTIONS OF A PROPOSAL

- *Cover sheet*
- *Abstract*
- *Table of contents*
- *Introduction.* Summary of problem, proposed method of attack, expected outcomes, feasibility of solution; written in nontechnical language for wide readership.
- *Statement of problem.* Specific definition with reference to relevant literature, if necessary, to show gap between the state-of-the-art and proposed work.
- *Objectives.* Tied realistically to problem; measurable; usually expressed in numbered list.
- *Method of attack.* Convinces reader that your approach is reasonable, specifically directed to the objectives, suited to your resources in people and facilities; procedure may be expressed as steps in numbered list; technical; may include review of literature to show how proposed approach differs from that of other workers; shows that approach is distinct, has special features or innovations; often includes figures and tables; may discuss likelihood of success; persuades reader to trust you.
- *Justification.* The "please note" section; anticipates reader's questions not answered in earlier sections; reiterates significance of problem and proves *why you*; focuses particularly on advantages to the client or customer and benefits to accrue from work; section may be included in introduction to short proposal.
- *Resources.* Assures reader that adequate staff and facilities are available to carry out project as outlined; profiles chief workers (extended biographies may be attached in an appendix); describes lab or field sites, specialized equipment, library and computer capabilities as matched to the tasks.
- *Evaluation.* A list of criteria by which you'll know if your project has succeeded; may mention outside consultants as evaluators.

• *Budget.* Assigns dollar values to the tasks defined in the method of attack and to the resources discussed; often read first as, in effect, the quantitative abstract of the proposal; total budget is divided into categories and subcategories in a long budget; each entry may be numbered for ease of reference.
• *References*
• *Appendix*

Not all of these sections, of course, apply to all situations. Each section, however, mirrors the one before it. That is, once you have defined the problem, you need to state objectives that match the problem. The method of attack then matches these objectives. And so on.

GUIDELINES FOR WRITING

1. Make sure the core idea comes through. Don't be afraid to repeat it. State it in the abstract or executive summary, the introduction, the objectives, the justification, the closing sales pitch.

2. Think in the reader's terms. Psychological order dominates (see p. 33). Avoid a list of "I want" sentences; instead, structure material to show how the work will benefit the reader, will solve some problem the reader must solve.

3. Speak the reader's language. Use terms familiar to the reader or explain new ones that need to be introduced. Phrase concepts in the way the reader phrases them, particularly in the way they are phrased in an RFP or other form of the assignment.

4. Emphasize benefits. Use headings that reinforce the core idea. Don't use just "nonsystemic errors" but "*reduction* of nonsystemic errors." Provide captions for figures which emphasize the core idea and sell the customer who only skims the text and flips through the visuals.

5. Be positive. Instead of saying, "The antenna radiation patterns are 3 dB below specifications over 13 percent of the coverage area," say, "The antenna radiation patterns meet or surpass specifications over 87 percent of the coverage area: the remaining coverage is 3 dB below the specified limit."

6. Use the future tense for actions in the future and the present tense for general descriptions. The context of a proposal indicates contingency; the work depends on approval of the request and usually allocation of funds. So you need not introduce the condition in verbs ("The work *would be* done"). This usage indicates some lack of self-confidence and increases the sheer weight of words in the text.

7. Show, don't tell. Convince with hard facts. Avoid the usual proposal jargon, especially in biographical sketches of investigators and descriptions of equipment. These elements of a proposal often move from one context to another without any tailoring to the new reader or checks on appropriateness to the work at hand. Make the language and evidence particular.

Reports

The proposal is the start of something new; the report tells what happened. *Report* is a general term for an account of some activity and what it adds up to. The term is frequently used in industry and government. Reports can circulate inside and outside a company or agency; they can be issued in only one copy, for only one reader or, like company annual reports, in hundreds of thousands of copies for hundreds of thousands of stockholders. Reports are differentiated by their materials and readers. But they share a common purpose: to inform—and usually to convince or change someone's mind or get someone to act. Because of the differences, it's hard to give one checklist for writing. But here are some suggestions pertinent to all reports. An example of the context and plan for one report then follows.

GUIDELINES FOR WRITING

1. In a long report aimed at several readers, provide several points of access to different parts of the report that match different reader interests. Tables of contents and

informative section headings help to do this. Or provide different covering letters for the report that direct each reader to a different section or plan for reading.

2. Build in some redundancy of information in multiple-reader reports. Few readers will read straight through, and you want to make sure that all read the main points.

3. Exploit the possibilities of visuals in the text and an appendix to convey the details of a financial or technical discussion. You may need to include some raw data to support conclusions, but keep it from bogging down the text.

4. Unless you anticipate strong reader opposition, give the answer up front. Avoid simply reporting on what you did in the order in which you did it, from the moment you set up a folder or interviewed the first person in the survey. That's like a description of a football game beginning with the kickoff and proceeding play by play to the final whistle. Readers want to know the score first.

5. Brief all readers, no matter what their interests or backgrounds, in a general introduction. The introduction summarizes your assessment of the communications context and suggests at broad scale the map of the report to follow.

CONTEXT AND PLAN FOR A FINAL REPORT: EXAMPLE

Context

The context is a report on a survey of mass rail transit in Philadelphia.

WRITER A consulting firm.

READERS Multiple—see figure 2.3. The *primary* reader is the federal Department of Transportation (DOT) which funded the study. Those at DOT who will read the report include program managers, financial officers, and the Assistant Secretary of Transportation. Some readers are economists, some engineers, some political scientists, and some political appointees with no background in any of these areas. Before the report reaches DOT, other *immediate* readers at the consulting firm—the writer's boss, other members of the project team, an in-house editor—will read and approve the report. *Secondary* readers who may respond to the recommendations in the report include other federal agencies, local authorities whose operations might be affected, the press, Congress and other oversight groups who monitor the use of federal funds, and interested bystanders who order the report through the National Technical Information Service.

PURPOSE   To report on a study of the economics and energy efficiency of high-speed mass rail transportation in the Philadelphia area and recommend increased DOT funding for mass transit projects.

MATERIAL

- results of a survey of over 50,000 commuters in Philadelphia
- results of a two-year study of rail, bus, and auto costs in Philadelphia
- calculations of costs and rider usage
- projections of effects of different DOT funding levels

DOCUMENT FORM   Final report, no particular specifications.

CONTROL STATEMENT   The Philadelphia Area Transit Survey shows that high-speed, mass rail transportation in established cities is more energy efficient and potentially cheaper than automobile and bus transportation in moving commuters between home and work and thus DOT should increase funding for mass transit.

Plan

Here's a plan that expands the control statement and indicates the broad divisions of the report:

I. Introduction—mass transit in American cities
II. The Philadelphia Area Transit Survey (PATS)
    A. Description of project
    B. Profile of the Philadelphia commuter
    C. Energy use in the Philadelphia commuter rail system
    D. Costs of the Philadelphia commuter rail system
III. Conclusions concerning energy and economics
IV. Detailed recommendations for DOT funding over five years
Appendix A: raw data on commuter survey
Appendix B: raw data on comparative costs of rail and private auto travel

The intention here is to present the information gathered in the PATS study to argue for increased federal spending. Each section supports and amplifies the assertions contained in the control statement. Each section requires a detailed plan. Here is one for part II.B:

II.B Profile of the Philadelphia commuter
    1. General summary of the commuter's typical characteristics: demographics, distance between work and home, frequency of travel, attitudes toward commuting.
    2. Demographics: age, sex, marital status, educational level, occupation, mean income.
    3. Distance between work and home: Chestnut Hill—West Line, Main Line, Media Line, Wilmington Line.
    4. Frequency of travel
    5. Attitudes toward commuting

Section 1 provides an overview, probably in a single paragraph beginning "PATS shows that the average Philadelphia commuter is. . . ." Sections 2 through 4 expand on each of the major points in the profile: demographics, distance between work and home, frequency of travel, and attitudes toward commuting. Within those, further divisions are made, as in section 3, which is divided into separate discussions for each major rail line serving the city. The level of detail in the plan varies, but each section supports and explains those to which it is subordinate in the plan.

Articles

Unlike a report, which is an object by itself, an article exists with other articles in a published form—in a journal or magazine. An article must meet the editor's specifications for maximum length, styling of references, form of presentation of text and visuals, and sometimes structuring of information. An article also competes with other articles in the issue for the reader's eye, and thus must have a title and first sentence that attract (and hold) attention. Reports circulate through a company to people with widely different interests and may emphasize local issues. An article circulates to the author's peers, people with similar interests and shared professional understandings. It emphasizes particular theoretical or practical information these colleagues might want to know. The article may describe a contribution to new knowledge. Or it may provide a new perspective, a better understanding of the profession. It may be a tutorial: practical advice on solving a problem. Journals often set up sections devoted to certain categories of information. You need to be familiar with these designations—and those of the journal in general—so that you can shape your material to the editor's and readers' interests. Figure 5.4 is the "Information for Contributors" page of *The Journal of Immunology*.[2] Learn similar pertinent information for the journal you are interested in submitting a manuscript to.

---

2. *The Journal of Immunology*, April 1981. The Williams and Wilkins Co., Baltimore. Reprinted with permission.

Figure 5.4
Sample instructions to authors of a journal article

The Journal of Immunology®

INFORMATION FOR CONTRIBUTORS

Manuscripts should be sent to:

The Journal of Immunology
Scripps Clinic and Research Foundation
La Jolla, CA 92037

Each manuscript submitted for publication must be accompanied by a check, money order, or purchase order for $50 in U.S. currency, payable to *The Journal of Immunology* at the address above. This charge is to cover the cost of processing manuscripts. The editorial review will not be initiated until this payment is received.

If the manuscript is published, it will become the sole property of The Williams & Wilkins Company, and all rights in copyright reserved to The Williams & Wilkins Company. The corresponding author may sign the Copyright Assignment form for all authors of the manuscript when it is accepted.

The length of the manuscript should be commensurate with the scientific content. The chief criteria for acceptance are quality, originality, clarity, and brevity.

INSTRUCTIONS FOR PREPARATION OF MANUSCRIPT

The original and 2 copies (legible carbon, mimeograph, or photo- copy), including *abstract, references, legends, figures,* and *illustrations,* must be typed **DOUBLE SPACED** (at least ³/₁₆ in. or 5-mm spacing from the bottom of one line to the top of a capital of a succeeding line) on one side of 8½ × 11 in. paper of good quality.

FOLLOW THIS FORMAT

1. *Running title* not to exceed 60 characters, typed double spaced on a separate page.

2. *Full title* typed double spaced on a separate page.

3. *Authors' full names* (first name, middle initial(s), surname) and affiliations typed double spaced on a separate page.

4. *Footnotes* (e.g., source of support, abbreviations if used, correspondence address, current address, unpublished references, etc.) typed double spaced on a separate page from the rest of the manuscript, but all footnotes may be typed on the same page.

5. *Abstract* typed double spaced on a separate page.

6. *Acknowledgment* immediately after the text, typed double spaced. *Grant support* should *not be included* in the *Acknowledgment* but should be cited as a footnote to the title.

7. *References* numbered as they appear in the text and listed in this format:

1. Kindt, T. J., and W. J. Mandy. 1972. Recombination of genes coding for constant and variable regions of immunoglobulin heavy chains. J. Immunol. 108:1110.

References typed double spaced and *not* on the same page with other material of the manuscript.

Only papers that have been accepted for publication should be listed in the references (i.e., articles that are already paginated or in press). Manuscripts in preparation, unpublished observations, and personal communications should be referred to as such in the text; completed manuscripts that have been submitted for publication may be cited as a footnote to the text. If such information is in press appropriate changes can be made in galley.

8. *Abbreviations* used and their meanings, typed double spaced, in one paragraph on a separate sheet (or on the page with other footnotes).

9. *Tables* typed double spaced on separate pages; legends and footnotes typed double spaced.

10. *Figures* (illustrations and photomicrographs) on glossy paper (in triplicate) and *not mounted*; legends typed double spaced on page(s) separate from the rest of the manuscript.

Figures should be carefully marked on the reverse side with figure number, first author's name, and orientation (top). Graphs should be in black ink on unlined or blue lined paper. If graphs exceed 9 x 12 in. in size, they must be accompanied by glossy photographic reproductions within that size. For photomicrographs a better grade of paper may be used at additional cost, up to $100 for a single page. Estimates can be obtained when the manuscript is accepted for publication. Estimates for color photomicrographs are also available.

11. *Position of tables and figures* in the text indicated on the left margin of the page.

12. *Culture medium components* used in experiments should be listed so that sufficient data to reproduce reported results are available. This information may be supplied in the *Abbreviations* footnote, in a table listing all components, by referring to a published article containing the information, or by identifying the commercial source that supplies the specific medium if components are listed by the supplier.

MANUSCRIPTS THAT DO NOT CONFORM TO THESE SPECIFICATIONS MAY NOT BE ACCEPTED, AT THE EDITOR'S DISCRETION

The *Communication* is a brief, definitive, and complete paper on a subject that is timely, important, novel, and of compelling interest to a large number of readers. It should not exceed 2 printed pages in length, including a summary (not required), references, tables, and figures. It is subject to the usual refereeing procedure. *If accepted, publication will not be accelerated.*

Letter to the Editor. Letters, which will be printed at the Editor's discretion, are responses to articles that have been published in *The Journal of Immunology* and should relate to scientific matters.

Opinion. This is an invited brief summary and commentary of a controversial subject of broad interest to immunologists.

Workshops. The Journal of Immunology will publish abstracts of workshops that have been refereed by program committees of the workshops. These will be accepted if each abstract is prepared for photocopy, i.e., typed single spaced on a separate page. Charges will be the full cost of each printed page.

Page Charges. Authors will be charged $45 for each printed page of an article or a Communication published in 1981. Accepted manuscripts will be published only after commitment by the author(s) or financial officer of their institution to pay such page charges. Under exceptional circumstances, page charges will be waived if deemed appropriate by an adjudicating committee of the Editorial Board.

Reprints. Reprints must be ordered in advance. A form showing the cost of reprints, together with an order slip, is sent with the galley proof. No more than 1000 reprints of any article may be purchased. The invoice for reprints will include the page charges.

GUIDELINES FOR WRITING

1. Take time to develop an effective title.

• Arrange key words early in the title:
Poor: *A Study of the Effects of Coffee on the Development of Heartburn*
Better: *Coffee and Heartburn: A Possible Causal Link*
• For professionals, give the answer in the title:
A Queuing System to Determine Priorities of Passengers on Overbooked Flights
• For popular readers, build motivation in the title:
How Much Is It Worth to You Not to Go to Houston? (for an article on overbooked flights)
Is Stress Killing You?
• Where appropriate, consider the possibilities of full-sentence titles:
Proven Computer Architecture Reduces Risks
• Keep modifiers in line:
A Logical Work Breakdown Structure (It's hard to tell what's breaking down.)
Comparison of Dried Milk Preparations for Babies on Sale in Seven European Countries (The milk is on sale, not the babies.)
• Make sure all necessary words are expressed:
Fluctuation of Quail in Northern Missouri, 1980–1985 (This sounds like an article about nervous quail. Instead, it's about fluctuations in *population*, a term that should be in the title.)
• Watch for unwanted connotations:
Views Men Have of Women in Labor (This article is about women in the labor force; labor has an alternate connotation for women.)
Architects Lose Jobs as Building Falls Off (One hopes no building fell off; if so, perhaps the architects should lose their jobs!)
The Effect of Free Radicals and Other Foreign Agents on Red Cells (This title is fine for biologists, but would be misleading in a journal of broader circulation.)
• Don't try to make the title an abstract. Some technical articles in particular have overly long titles.
• When the setting is appropriate, be clever. You might use a pun:

Big Steel Recasts Itself

Puns and other word play appear frequently in titles like this one from the *Wall Street Journal,* which in general features fine titles. Here's a sample, a full-sentence title to an article about the plain English campaign in Washington:

Modes to Defuzzify Officialese Impact Minutely Resultwise

2. Build an enticing and informative first sentence—the lead. Here are some possibilities:

• *Comparison:* "In a sense, the pathologist and physiologist approach an endocrinological problem from opposite sides."
• *Narrative detail:* "Makers of office equipment and computers are dreaming of a paperless office of the future, where workers shuffle information electronically and executives confer via video screens with far-flung colleagues." (*Wall Street Journal,* 3/13/81, p. 1)
• *Prediction:* "The economics of building computers are changing." (*Business Week,* 3/23/81, p. 82)
• *Contrast of known/unknown:* "There can be nothing simpler than an elementary particle: it is an indivisible shard of matter, without internal structure and without detectable shape or size." (*Scientific American,* April 1981, p. 48)

• 3. Follow the lead with an introductory section that gives readers a framework for understanding your main point. The first paragraph in particular shapes the reader's attitude toward the article. Include the following:

• a statement concerning what the article is about and will do for the reader—your control statement.
• any brief background necessary for the reader to understand the statement (definitions, reference to the literature). Save elaboration on the background for the second section of the article.
• scope of the article. State what is covered, and perhaps what is not covered, if the reader might expect something you don't want to discuss. Indicate your emphasis and point of view.
• plan of organization of the article, probably the last sentence in the section: "This article discusses four forces of change in savings and loan institutions: technology, consumerism, competition, and inflation."

4. Envision the whole in print. Be aware of the factor of reduction in print. Make sure that elements in visuals—lines in drawings, curves on charts, shadings in photos—are bold enough in the original to stand out when the originals are reduced for publication. If you have too many curves, for example, or two curves are too close together, the result in print may be a simple muddle. Paragraph size is also reduced. That means that a series of short paragraphs in typescript may seem like only a list in print. Adjust paragraph length to take reduction.

Dissertations and Theses

Dissertations and theses differ in many ways from other forms we have discussed. Memos, letters, and reports, for example, circulate in both organizational and professional circles. Dissertations (a term we use to cover theses as well) are strictly academic. Whereas one may write hundreds—perhaps more than a thousand—memos in a lifetime, those who choose to write dissertations generally write only one. The first time is usually the only time. Moreover, the content of a dissertation focuses more on what the writer did or thought than on what the reader ought to do on the basis of that activity—except, of course, to approve the dissertation. It is a document aimed more to certify the writer than to inform the reader. For all these reasons, a dissertation is often unwieldy, with many headings and subheadings. Thus Ph.D. recipients have to apply for a year or so of leave to turn the dissertation into something publishable—something readable in the field.

Of course, dissertations need not be unreadable. Much depends on the taste and direction of the adviser, whose desires set the framework for both content and style of presentation. Usually, too, there is a committee of readers for the dissertation. If members are at war with each other, a writer may be caught in the crossfire, endlessly revising to suit one reader, only to be rebuffed by another. Writing for multiple audiences in organizations is often less complex than writing for eccentrics on a committee the adviser has let get out of hand.

A reasonable adviser, however, can encourage readability. To accomplish this goal, the writer, too, must keep certain items in mind.

GUIDELINES FOR WRITING

1. At the outset, obtain a copy of your department's or university's requirements for format of the dissertation. These are usually detailed to facilitate binding of texts to be shelved in the library and reproduction by University Microfilms. You court disaster if you don't pay attention to such mundane matters as the size of margins, number of copies, and form and placement of documentation.

2. Think about the dissertation as you conduct research. Collect lab, field, or reading notes in a form that eases the writing. Remember the form (and length) of the dissertation and adjust your work accordingly as you proceed.

3. This may well be the longest document you have written to date—and the longest you'll write for years to come. To assure some coherence among chapters and not submit merely a series of term papers end to end, you will need a detailed plan for the document. Check out the plan well in advance of the writing with your adviser and committee. Try to troubleshoot any objections in the planning stage rather than waiting until you've written a chapter to find that your idea is not what was wanted.

4. The plan for the dissertation may be established by custom or convention in your field. Most such documents include a review of literature that shows the writer to be up to date in the subject. For original research, especially in science and technical fields, it may also entail sections on materials and methods, results, discussion, and conclusions. Within the sections, however, you need to organize your unique material to show its potential and your cleverness. The sequence and chapter breaks must be clear.

5. In selecting materials for the dissertation, don't be seduced into irrelevancies, even if the information was hard to come by or particularly amusing. Focus unremittingly on the goal: an approved dissertation that earns you the long-sought letters after your name.

6. With the plan clearly in mind (or perhaps clearly posted on a bulletin board over your desk), write the dissertation chapter by chapter, and seek approval chapter by chapter. Don't wait until the end for approvals.

7. Following preliminary readings by your adviser, carefully review his or her comments to pick out special likes and dislikes in mechanics, style, and organization. Many students suffer the agony of multiple revisions merely to please a reader's quirk in choice of words (for example, *which* vs. *that*), use of punctuation (some love colons, some detest them), or paragraph length. Notice these preferences early and accommodate your writing to them.

Selected Sources on Writing

Adelstein, Michael. *Contemporary Business Writing*. New York: Random House, 1971.

Andrews, Deborah C. and Margaret D. Blickle. *Technical Writing: Principles and Forms*. 2d ed. New York: Macmillan, 1982.

Barzun, Jacques. *Simple and Direct: A Rhetoric for Writers*. New York: Harper & Row, 1975.

Berenson, Conrad and Raymond Colton. *Research and Report Writing for Business and Economics*. New York: Random House, 1971.

Brusaw, Charles T., Gerald J. Alred, and Walter E. Oliu. *Handbook of Technical Writing*. New York: St. Martin, 1976.

——. *The Business Writer's Handbook*. New York: St. Martin, 1976.

Corbett, Edward P. J. *The Little English Handbook*. 2d ed. New York: Wiley, 1977.

Day, Robert. *How to Write and Publish a Scientific Paper*. Philadelphia: ISI Press, 1979.

Flesch, Rudolf. *The ABC of Style: A Guide to Plain English*. New York: Harper & Row, 1980.

Gunning, Robert. *Techniques of Clear Writing*. Rev. ed. New York: McGraw-Hill, 1968.

Kapp, Reginald O. *The Presentation of Technical Information*. New York: Macmillan, 1957.

Mathes, J. C. and Dwight W. Stevenson. *Designing Technical Reports*. Indianapolis: Bobbs-Merrill, 1976.

Menzel, Donald H., Howard Mumford Jones, and Lyle G. Boyd. *Writing a Technical Paper*. New York: McGraw-Hill, 1961.

Rathbone, Robert. *Communicating Technical Information*. Reading, MA: Addison-Wesley, 1972.

Sigband, Norman. *Communication for Management and Business*. 2d ed. New York: Scott Foresman, 1976.

Strunk, William and E. B. White. *The Elements of Style*. 3d ed. New York: Macmillan, 1979.

Trelease, Sam F. *How to Write Scientific and Technical Papers.* Cambridge, MA: MIT Press, 1969.

Turabian, Kate L. *Manual for Writers of Term Papers, Theses, and Dissertations.* 4th ed. Chicago: University of Chicago Press, 1973.

U.S. General Accounting Office. *From Auditing to Editing.* Washington: Government Printing Office, 1974.

U.S. Government Printing Office. *Style Manual.* Rev. ed. Washington: Government Printing Office, 1973.

U.S. Treasury Department. *Effective Revenue Writing 2.* Rev. ed. Washington: Government Printing Office, 1962.

Weiss, Allen. *Write What You Mean: A Handbook of Business Communication.* New York: American Management Association, 1978.

· INDEX ·

I.C.C. LIBRARY